From My Heart

RICKY CLEMONS

PUBLISHED BY FIEDLI PUBLISHING, INC.

Copyright ©2021, Ricky Clemons
ALL RIGHTS RESERVED.

No part of this publication may be reproduced, stored in a retrieval system, or transmitted in any form or by any means—electronic, mechanical, photo-copy, recording, or any other—except for brief quotation in reviews, without the prior permission of the author or publisher.

ISBN: 978-1-955622-80-6

Published by

Fideli Publishing, Inc.
119 W. Morgan St.
Martinsville, IN 46151
www.FideliPublishing.com

Table of Contents

From My Heart 1

That Split Second Between Life and Death 5

The Heart in Your Chest is Small 7

Having Faith In You, O Lord 14

I See You 16

Nature and Human Nature 18

People We Don't Know 20

I Want to Keep My Eyeson Jesus 22

Actions 28

Good Men and Good Women 30

If People Can't Control You and Me 32

There is Nothing Like Love 34

How Can Our Hearts Be Right with the Lord? 37

The Beginning 39

A Mystery 43

Passing Through 45

This World 47

True Freedom 58

Use Your 60

Of Their Own Race 62

There is No Good Life In 65

Many people believe 68

Will Use Jesus's Name	70
Oh Lord, You Always Know	72
It can make us feel good	74
If We Don'tPut Our Trust In The Lord	76
The Battle of Good Against Evil	78
Everybody Needs God	80
Common People	82
Don't Look Down on People	84
The Devil Knows	86
Something Always Comes Up	87
First Impression Shouldn't Always Be Lasting Impressions	89
Imaginary	91
Doing Your Holy Will, O Lord	94
Living an Honest Life	96
It Didn't Happen Overnight	98
Oh Lord, You know	100
Eternal Life To Look Forward To	102
In the Name of Jesus	104
Jesus is Like	106
Jesus Can	108
What Have We Black People Done to You White People?	110
The Black Will	115
The Black Dream	118
There Is Nothing Good About The Devil	122
Make Something Good Out of Something Bad	125
We Christians Can't Sit Back	127

From My Heart

I am trying my best to write prose poetry from my heart to share with you.

I want to be real with you in my prose poetry that I love to write.

I try my best to write what I feel.

I try my best to write what I see.

I try my best to write what I experienced.

I try my best to write the truth.

Whatever prose poem The Lord inspires me to write, I must share it with others, so they can be blessed by my poetry.

I believe by faith that some people will be blessed by my inspiring prose poetry.

I believe that some people can relate to my prose poetry.

I love to write prose poetry from my heart because I want to be real with others, whether they are blessed or not blessed by what I write.

I believe by faith that the Lord inspires me to write prose poetry so that I can help myself keep my faith in Him.

I believe by faith that the Lord inspires me to write prose poetry to help others keep their faith in him.

Whatever poem The Lord inspires me to write, I know that I must write it.

Some prose poems the Lord inspires me to write are easy to write.

Some prose poems the Lord inspires me to write are hard to write.

Some prose poems the Lord inspires me to write are ones I don't want to write.

I believe by faith that the Lord gives me good prose poems to write and share with others whether they like it or not after they read my prose poetry.

My prose poetry is from my heart and I need the Lord to make it real.

I want my prose poetry to be real and true from my heart.

If you read my prose poetry, I pray and hope that you will understand what I feel, what I see and what I experienced to share with you.

I am sharing with you my faith in the Lord.

I am sharing with you my relationship with the Lord.

I am sharing with you my testimonies about the Lord.

I am sharing with you my hope in the Lord.

I am sharing with you my love for the Lord.

I am sharing with you that I know that I need the Lord in my life.

I wouldn't want to write prose poetry if I couldn't write it from my heart.

Some people may like my prose poetry and some people may not like my prose poetry, even though the Lord inspired me to write it to help others to see the truth.

My prose poetry helps me to see the truth about myself and I believe that it will help other people to see the truth about themselves.

The Lord Jesus Christ, who I believe in, is the Living Truth and he surely knows how to show you and me the truth about ourselves.

The Lord has shown me a lot of truth about myself in the prose poems that he has inspired me to write.

If you read my prose poetry, you will have a good idea about who I am in the Lord.

The Lord has brought me a long way and I know that I still have a long way to go in the Lord.

On my Christian journey that is not easy, I want to share my prose poetry about my Lord with you so that you can read and hopefully understand my walk with the Lord even though it may be different from your walk with the Lord.

Prose poetry from my heart is what I love to share with others who I want to be real with.

I worship a real Lord and Savior who is always real with you and me.

You and I don't have to be educated to be real.

I can only be me and you can only be you, but I hope that the prose poetry that I write will influence you to not judge me if it is not up on your spiritual level.

My prose poetry about the Lord is plain and simple, for me to be who I am from my heart.

I can only give you my realness, I know that you will either accept it or not accept it.

The most important thing to me is that the Lord accepts me being real in my prose poetry that is never worthless to him, even if some people don't like my prose poetry.

I am learning so much that everyone will not be blessed by what you and I do for the Lord.

I am very thankful unto the Lord that there are some people who are blessed by my prose poetry about the Lord.

My prose poetry is not about causing anyone to feel good when you read it.

My prose poetry is about causing you and me to be convicted of our sins.

No one feels good about being convicted of the wrongs that we do.

I love writing serious prose poetry because we are living in serious times and I know Jesus Christ is coming back again.

Jesus is serious about saving you and me from our sins.

Feel-good poetry may be for those who are not real with themselves about accepting the truth of needing to be convicted and converted by the Holy Spirit.

All of my prose poetry is spiritual from the Holy Spirit who reveals to us the whole truth.

Some of my prose poetry steps on my toes to convict me of my sins.

I don't want to share prose poetry with you if it doesn't do anything good for me.

Pastors can preach sermons and bible school teachers can spread the Gospel of Jesus Christ.

But if the pastor's sermon doesn't do the pastor any good then why would the pastor want their sermons to do you and me any good?

It's the same thing with my poetry.

My prose poetry about the Lord does me good and I believe that it will do some other people good too.

The Lord hasn't failed me yet in my prose poetry.

To God be the glory.

That Split Second Between Life and Death

On a weekday in the early afternoon, I left my house and got in my car.

My mind was on going to the T-Mobile store to get my phone back in service.

I also had my mind on getting my second covid-19 vaccine shot.

When I got in my car, I drove out of my parking space and entered onto the main road that leads to the upcoming traffic.

I stopped at the end of the road where I was supposed to wait until the traffic was clear.

I was a little impatient when a trash truck driver slowed down to turn off the road.

The trash truck driver drove close to me as I was on the opposite side of the main road that leads out.

Before the trash truck driver made his turn off of the road, I began to drive in front of him because I didn't see the oncoming traffic.

I truly thank the Lord that I drove out slowly and was able to quickly press down on the brakes to stop just in time before a speeding vehicle could hit me.

I believe that the Lord must have sent down an angel from heaven to force my feet down onto the brake pedal at the right time.

That angel came from Heaven a lot faster than the speed of light because it was just a split second between life and death that I was able to hit my brakes.

I didn't have time to think about hitting my break.

It was a miracle to me that my foot pressed down on the brake pedal really fast.

That very moment was like my life was moving in slow motion and that vehicle was moving fast, ready to hit my car and probably kill me.

The Lord showed me that it wasn't my time to leave here and join the dead.

The Lord showed me that no matter what good things I do, it's not enough to prolong my life if it's my time to join the dead.

The Lord showed me that he is the one who can truly shorten my life or prolong my life.

I am so happy that the Lord spared my life in that split second between life and death.

I am so glad that the Lord is not finished with me yet.

The devil wanted me to be hit by that speeding vehicle that I couldn't see because of the trash truck blocking the view.

If I had been in a big hurry to drive around the trash truck, I probably would have been killed.

The Lord was surely ahead of me to see that speeding vehicle that I didn't see coming my way.

The Lord sent down an angel from Heaven to force my foot down on the brake pedal in the split second between life and death.

The Lord showed me that everything is about His time and not my time.

I can make my time be short and surely not know when the Lord has the power to rule over my time and give me more time to live beyond a split-second between life and death.

I can easily take my life for granted when the Lord is so merciful and sees fit for me to live through this day that I don't deserve to see.

A split second between life and death can be a frightening experience, and if the Lord is in it, there will be a calmness in our spirit that the devil can't disturb.

The Heart in Your Chest is Small

The heart in your chest is small, but it can be gigantic in motives.

The heart in your chest is small, but it can be gigantic in intentions.

The heart in your chest is small, but it can be gigantic and feelings.

The heart in your chest is small, but it can be gigantic in goodness.

The heart in your chest is small, but it can be gigantic in kindness.

The heart in your chest is small, but it can be gigantic in pride.

The heart in your chest is small, but it can be gigantic in greed.

The heart in your chest is small, but it can be gigantic in mischief.

The heart in your chest is small, but it can be gigantic in fear.

The heart in your chest is small, but it can be gigantic in courage.

The heart in your chest is small, but it can be gigantic in pretense.

The heart in your chest is small, but it can be gigantic in realness.

The heart in your chest is small, but it can be gigantic in joy.

The heart in your chest is small, but it can be gigantic in greed.

The heart in your chest is small, but it can be gigantic in dedication.

The heart in your chest is small, but it can be gigantic in determination.

The heart in your chest is small, but it can be gigantic in truth.

The heart in your chest is small, but it can be gigantic in lies.

The heart in your chest is small, but it can be gigantic in deception.

The heart in your chest is small, but it can be gigantic in happiness.

The heart in your chest is small, but it can be gigantic in loneliness.

The heart in your chest is small, but it can be gigantic in security.

The heart in your chest is small, but it can be gigantic in insecurity.

The heart in your chest is small, but it can be gigantic in temperance.

The heart in your chest is small, but it can be gigantic in intemperance.

The heart in your chest is small, but it can be gigantic in humility.

The heart in your chest is small, but it can be gigantic in selfishness.

The heart in your chest is small, but it can be gigantic and selflessness.

The heart in your chest is small, but it can be gigantic and emotions.
The heart in your chest is small, but it can be gigantic in hate.

The heart in your chest is small, but it can be gigantic in rebellion.

The heart in your chest is small, but it can be gigantic in prejudice.

The heart in your chest is small, but it can be gigantic in injustice.

The heart in your chest is small, but it can be gigantic in justice.

The heart in your chest is small, but it can be gigantic in equality.

The heart in your chest is small, but it can be gigantic in inequality.

The heart in your chest is small, but it can be gigantic in wickedness.

The heart in your chest is small, but it can be gigantic in peace.

The heart in your chest is small, but it can be gigantic in strife.

The heart in your chest is small, but it can be gigantic in jealousy.

The heart in your chest is small, but it can be gigantic in lust.

The heart in your chest is small, but it can be gigantic in envy.

The heart in your chest is small, but it can be gigantic in hope in the Lord and Savior Jesus Christ.

The heart in your chest is small, but it can be gigantic in obedience unto the Lord Jesus Christ.

The heart in your chest is small, but it can be gigantic in believing in the Lord Jesus Christ.

The heart in your chest is small, but it can be gigantic in disobedience unto the Lord Jesus Christ.

The heart in your chest is small, but it can be gigantic in disbelief in the Lord Jesus Christ.

The heart in your chest is small, but it can be gigantic in honesty.

The heart in your chest is small, but it can be gigantic in dishonesty.

The heart in your chest is small, but it can be gigantic in loyalty.

The heart in your chest is small, but it can be gigantic in disloyalty.

The heart in your chest is small, but it can be gigantic in good choices.

The heart in your chest is small, but it can be gigantic in bad choices.

The heart in your chest is small, but it can be gigantic in heartache.

The heart in your chest is small, but it can be gigantic in unfaithfulness.

The heart in your chest is small, but it can be gigantic in discontentment.

The heart in your chest is small, but it can be gigantic in contentment.

The heart in your chest is small, but it can be gigantic in compassion.

The heart in your chest is small, but it can be gigantic in love.

The heart in your chest is small, but it can be gigantic in giving.

The heart in your chest is small, but it can be gigantic in rudeness.

The heart in your chest is small, but it can be gigantic in favor with God.

The heart in your chest is small, but it can be gigantic in in sincerity.

The heart in your chest is small, but it can be gigantic in in insincerity.

The heart in your chest is small, but it can be gigantic in forgiveness.

The heart in your chest is small, but it can be gigantic in unforgiveness.

The heart in your chest is small, but it can be gigantic in foolishness.

The heart in your chest is small, but it can be gigantic in loving the Lord Jesus Christ.

The heart in your chest is small, but it can be gigantic in not loving the Lord Jesus Christ.

The heart in your chest is small, but it can be gigantic in trusting in the Lord Jesus Christ.

The heart in your chest is small, but it can be gigantic in not trusting in the Lord Jesus Christ.

The heart in your chest is small, but it can pump blood through every vein in the body.

The heart in your chest is small, but it can be gigantic in sin all through the body.

The heart in your chest is small, but it can be gigantic in unrighteousness.

The heart in your chest is small, but it can be gigantic in the righteousness of Jesus Christ.

The heart in your chest is small, but it can be gigantic in wisdom from the Lord Jesus Christ.

The heart in your chest is small, but it can be gigantic in discernment from the Lord Jesus Christ.

The heart in your chest is small, but it can be gigantic in treason.

The heart in your chest is small, but it can be gigantic in betrayal that Judas did to Jesus Christ.

The heart in your chest is small, but it can be gigantic in guilt.

The heart in your chest is small, but it can be gigantic in blame.

The heart in your chest is small, but it can be gigantic in mistakes.

The heart in your chest is small, but it can be gigantic in lawlessness.

The heart in your chest is small, but it can be gigantic in experience.

The heart in your chest is small, but it can be gigantic in unpredictability.

The heart in your chest is small, but it can be gigantic in misinterpretation.

The heart in your chest is small, but it can be gigantic in interpretation.

The heart in your chest is small, but it can be gigantic in inexperience.

The heart in your chest is small, but it can be gigantic in the acceptance.

The heart in your chest is small, but it can be gigantic in rejection.

The heart in your chest is small, but it can be gigantic in judging.

The heart in your chest is small, but it can be gigantic in partiality.

The heart in your chest is small, but it can be gigantic in favoritism.

The heart in your chest is small, but it can be gigantic in transformation.

The heart in your chest is small, but it can be gigantic in achievement.

The heart in your chest is small, but it can be gigantic in victory.

The heart in your chest is small, but it can be gigantic in defensiveness.

The heart in your chest is small, but it can be gigantic in sharing.

The heart in your chest is small, but it can be gigantic in not sharing.

The heart in your chest is small, but it can be gigantic in silence.

The heart in your chest is small, but it can be gigantic in speaking up.

The heart in your chest is small, but it can be gigantic in schemes.

The heart in your chest is small, but it can be gigantic in disguise.

The heart in your chest is small, but it can be gigantic in disgust.

The heart in your chest is small, but it can be gigantic in moral corruption.

The heart in your chest is small, but it can be gigantic in moral decency.

The heart in your chest is small, but it can be gigantic in agreement.

The heart in your chest is small, but it can be gigantic in disagreement.

The heart in your chest is small, but it can be gigantic in pleasing God.

The heart in your chest is small, but it can be gigantic in displeasing God.

The heart in your chest is small, but it can be gigantic in recklessness.

The heart in your chest is small, but it can be gigantic in division.

The heart in your chest is small, but it can be gigantic in unity unto the Lord.

The heart in your chest is small, but it can be gigantic in changing for better or changing for worse.

The heart in your chest is small, but it can be gigantic in believing the truth or believing lies.

The heart in your chest is small, but it can be gigantic in being right or wrong.

The heart in your chest is small, but it can be gigantic in being good or bad.

The heart in your chest is small, but it can be gigantic in being warm-hearted or cold hearted.

The heart in your chest is small, but it can be gigantic in changing with the times.

The heart in your chest is small, but it can be gigantic in beauty or ugliness.

The heart in your chest is small, but it can be gigantic in a wish or reality.

The heart in your chest is small, but it can be gigantic in an idea or fact.

The heart in your chest is small, but it can be gigantic and crossing over boundaries.

The heart in your chest is small, but it can be gigantic in worshipping the Lord and Savior Jesus Christ or worshipping idols.

The heart in your chest is small, but it can be gigantic in greed.

The heart in your chest is small, but it can pump lifeblood through every vein in our bodies so you and I can live.

The heart in your chest is small, but it can keep you and me alive for many years.

The heart in your chest is small, but it can put up with you and me making it through some changes in life.

The heart in your chest is small, but it can be gigantic in changing the world for better or for worse.

The heart in your chest is small, but it can be gigantic in giving it all to God.

The heart in your chest is small, but it can be gigantic in not giving God the glory and the praise.

The heart in your chest is small, but it can be gigantic in superiority.

The heart in your chest is small, but it can be gigantic in manipulation.

The heart in your chest is small, but it can be gigantic in actions.

The heart in your chest is small, but it can be gigantic in the devil.

The heart in your chest is small, but it can be gigantic in God.

Having Faith In You, O Lord

Having faith in You, O Lord, keeps me going strong.

Having faith in You, O Lord, helps me to live in reality.

Having faith in You, O Lord, help me to do your holy will.

Having faith in You, O Lord, helps me to love everybody.

Having faith in You, O Lord, gives me something good to look forward to.

Having faith in You, O Lord, is the best thing in my life.

Having faith in You, O Lord, help me to keep my eyes on you.

Having faith in You, O Lord, makes me strong when I am weak.

Having faith in You, O Lord, helps me to love you and keep your Commandments.

Having faith in You, O Lord, gives me encouragement.

Having faith in You, O Lord, motivates me to live right.

Having faith in You, O Lord, helps me to be honest with everybody.

Having faith in You, O Lord, lifts me up when I am feeling down

Having faith in You, O Lord, helps me to meditate on you.

Having faith in You, O Lord, helps me to read your holy word.

Having faith in You, O Lord, brings me back to You when I am feeling lost.

Having faith in You, O Lord, helps me to think on spiritual things.

Having faith in You, O Lord, helps me to walk on Your straight and narrow road.

Having faith in You, O Lord, helps me to face up to my trials.

Having faith in You, O Lord, helps me to finish what I started.

Having faith in You, O Lord, helps me to not be too hard on myself.

Having faith in You, O Lord, helps me to not be hard on others.

Having faith in You, O Lord, gives me hope in this sinful world.

Having faith in You, O Lord, helps me to know that I have a lot to live for.

Having faith in You, O Lord, helps me to stay awake spiritually to be ready for Your second coming back to this world.

I See You

My Lord Jesus Christ, I see You telling me the truth in Your holy word that I must read for myself.

Oh, my Lord, I see you opening up my blind spiritual eyes so that I can see You are the living truth.

My Lord Jesus Christ, I see You telling me to pray without ceasing in Your holy word.

I know that whenever I pray to You, You will lift me up from the pits of stress and cause me to feel a lot better so my mind can shine in Your glory.

My Lord Jesus Christ, I see You talking to me in Your holy word and counseling me to deny myself, pick up my cross and follow you one day at a time.

I see you, my Lord Jesus Christ, talking to me so kindly with authority.

You get through to me so I can see that You love me and will save my soul for believing in You.

My Lord Jesus Christ, I see you quenching my thirsty soul in Your holy word that lets me know that You are the living waters of life that I can drink and You will refresh my soul.

Oh, my Lord and Savior Jesus Christ, I see you feeding my hungry soul with your holy word that lets me know that you are the bread of life that will never get stale and will never mold.

Only you, my Lord Jesus, can fill up my hungry soul with the truth and set me free from spiritual starvation.

Oh, my Lord, I see You encouraging me to hold on to You and Your holy word because You are the word of God and the word was made flesh and lived among sinners like me.

My Lord Jesus Christ, I see You in Your holy word from the book of Genesis to the book of Revelations where all the prophets of God and all the disciples point to You to fulfill their existence and divine missions from You.

My Lord Jesus Christ, I see You giving me spiritual strength, mental strength and the physical strength to make it through the day.

Your holy word backs me up, because You are Your holy word that fills up my life with hope and faith in You from day to day.

Oh, my Lord Jesus Christ, I see You telling me to love You and obey You in Your holy word that You fulfilled before You created the heavens and the earth.

Nature and Human Nature

Nature can give us peace of mind.

Nature can look so good in our eyes.

Human nature can look so corrupt.

Nature can heal our broken spirits.

Human nature can cause us to get sick.

Nature can be so quiet all day long.

Human nature can be so noisy all day long and all night long.

Human nature can discourage us and make us do evil.

Nature can help us to be patient.

Human nature can cause us to be hasty.

Nature can give us its unchangeable presence to help us get through the day.

Human nature can give us changeable ways and put a damper on our day.

Nature can slow us down so we can enjoy life.

Human nature can cause us to move too fast so we don't see that life is what we make of it one day at a time.

Nature can cause us to not overreact when problems come our way.

Human nature can cause us to overreact and say or do something that is wrong.

Nature can help us to look into our own hearts and see our true selves.

Nature can show us that there is a God who created nature.

Human nature can cause us to believe that there is no God.

Nature can draw us to God.

Human nature can cause us to pull away from God.

Human nature can confuse our minds and make us think about bad things.

Nature can help us to wise up and do what is right.

Human nature can cause us to be fools and deceive us into thinking we have our lives together without living our lives unto Jesus Christ.

Nature is not sinful.

Human nature is sinful every day.

People We Don't Know

It's easy to be opinionated about people we don't know.

It's easy to assume things about people we don't know.

It's easy to pretend with people we don't know.

It takes time to get to know people we don't know.

There are billions of people in this world that we will never get to know.

The Lord knows all people we don't know.

It's easy to think bad things about people we don't know.

It's easy to say bad things about people we don't know.

It's easy to misunderstand people we don't know.

It's easy to mistreat people we don't know.

It's easy to have ill feelings about people we don't know.

It's easy to laugh at people we don't know.

It's easy to joke about people we don't know.

It's easy to not be happy for people we don't know.

It's easy to not smile at people we don't know.

It's easy to not talk to people we don't know.

It's easy to not trust people we don't know.

There are some people who will not talk to people they don't know.

There are some people who will talk bad about people they don't know.

There are some people who will assume things about people they don't know.

There are some people who will think bad thoughts about people they don't know.

It's easy to put down people we don't know.

There are some people who will put down people they don't know.

There are billions of people in this world and the Lord knows everybody and will judge them all fairly.

It's easy to walk by people we don't know.

It's easy to not pay attention to people we don't know.

It's easy to not help people we don't know.

Some people will not help people they don't know.

There are some people who will not pay attention to people they don't know.

It's easy to reject people we don't know.

It's easy to lie to people we don't know.

It's easy to be afraid of people we don't know.

It's easy for the Lord to love everybody.

It's easy for the Lord to save everybody from being lost in sin if we all confess and repent and turn to Him.

I Want to Keep My Eyes on Jesus

I don't want to keep my eyes on people who make mistakes.
I want to keep my eyes on Jesus; He makes no mistakes.
I don't want to keep my eyes on people who have flaws.
I want to keep my eyes on Jesus, who has no flaws.
I don't want to keep my eyes on people who can say something wrong.
I want to keep my eyes on Jesus, who can't say anything wrong.
I don't want to keep my eyes on people who can do something wrong.
I want to keep my eyes on Jesus, who can't do anything wrong.
I don't want to keep my eyes on people who I can't put all my trust in.
I want to keep my eyes on Jesus, who I can put all my trust in.
I don't want to keep my eyes on people who can let me down.
I want to keep my eyes on Jesus, who will never let me down.
I don't want to keep my eyes on people who can tell me a lie.
I want to keep my eyes on Jesus, who can't lie to me.
I don't want to keep my eyes on people who can deceive me.
I want to keep my eyes on Jesus, who will never deceive me.
I don't want to keep my eyes on people who can disappoint me.
I want to keep my eyes on Jesus, who will never disappoint me.
I don't want to keep my eyes on people who can talk bad about me.
I want to keep my eyes on Jesus, who will never talk bad about me.
I don't want to keep my eyes on people who can lie about me.
I want to keep my eyes on Jesus, who will never lie about me.

I don't want to keep my eyes on people who can cheat me.

I want to keep my eyes on Jesus, who will never cheat me.

I don't want to keep my eyes on people who can use me.

I want to keep my eyes on Jesus, who will never use me.

I don't want to keep my eyes on people who can hate me.

I want to keep my eyes on Jesus, who will never hate me.

I don't want to keep my eyes on people who can dislike me.

I want to keep my eyes on Jesus, who will never dislike me.

I don't want to keep my eyes on people who can fail me.

I want to keep my eyes on Jesus, who will never fail me.

I don't want to keep my eyes on people who can give me injustice.

I want to keep my eyes on Jesus, who will always give me justice.

I don't want to keep my eyes on people who can misunderstand me.

I want to keep my eyes on Jesus, who will never misunderstand me.

I don't want to keep my eyes on people who can kill me.

I want to keep my eyes on Jesus, who will never kill me.

I don't want to keep my eyes on people who can steal from me.

I want to keep my eyes on Jesus who will never steal from me.

I don't want to keep my eyes on people who can hurt me.

I want to keep my eyes on Jesus who will never hurt me.

I don't want to keep my eyes on people who can be opinionated about me.

I want to keep my eyes on Jesus, who will never be opinionated about me.

I don't want to keep my eyes on people who can change on me.

I want to keep my eyes on Jesus, who will never change on me.

I don't want to keep my eyes on people who can leave me or forsake me.

I want to keep my eyes on Jesus, who will never leave me or forsake me.

I don't want to keep my eyes on people who can reject me.

I want to keep my eyes on Jesus, who will never reject me.

I don't want to keep my eyes on people who can take me the wrong way.

I want to keep my eyes on Jesus, who will never take me the wrong way.

I don't want to keep my eyes on people who can ignore me.

I want to keep my eyes on Jesus, who will never ignore me.

I don't want to keep my eyes on people who can trick me.

I want to keep my eyes on Jesus, who will never trick me.

I don't want to keep my eyes on people who can want to control me.

I want to keep my eyes on Jesus, who will never control me.

I don't want to keep my eyes on people who can want to fight me.

I want to keep my eyes on Jesus, who will never fight me.

I don't want to keep my eyes on people who may not be real with me.

I want to keep my eyes on Jesus, who is always real with me.

I don't want to keep my eyes on people who can see me and can act like they don't see me.

I want to keep my eyes on Jesus, who sees me and lets me know that He sees me.

I don't want to keep my eyes on people who can hear me and can act like they don't hear me.

I want to keep my eyes on Jesus, who hears me and lets me know that He hears me.

I don't want to keep my eyes on people who can oppress me.

I want to keep my eyes on Jesus, who will never oppress me.

I don't want to keep my eyes on people who can depress me.

I want to keep my eyes on Jesus, who can never depress me.

I don't want to keep my eyes on people who can cause me to get sick.

I want to keep my eyes on Jesus, who will never cause me to get sick.

I don't want to keep my eyes on people who are not perfect.

I want to keep my eyes on Jesus, who is perfect and without sin.

I don't want to keep my eyes on people who have sins to confess and repent of.

I want to keep my eyes on Jesus, who can save me from my sins.

I don't want to keep my eyes on people who have no heaven to put me in.

I want to keep my eyes on Jesus, who has a heaven to put me in.

I don't want to keep my eyes on people who can mess things up.

I want to keep my eyes on Jesus, who will never mess anything up.

I don't want to keep my eyes on people who can set me up for a fall.

I want to keep my eyes on Jesus, who will never set me up for a fall.

I don't want to keep my eyes on people who can be jealous of me.

I want to keep my eyes on Jesus, who wants to give me the best.

I don't want to keep my eyes on people who can act like they're better than me.

I want to keep my eyes on Jesus, who created me wonderfully made in His image.

I want to always keep my eyes on Jesus Christ, my Lord and Savior.

I don't want to keep my eyes on people who can pretend to be something they are not.

I don't want to keep my eyes on people who can mock me.

I want to keep my eyes on Jesus, who will never mock me.

I don't want to keep my eyes on people who can break my heart.

I want to keep my eyes on Jesus, who will never break my heart.

I don't want to keep my eyes on people who can tell me one thing and then do another thing.

I want to keep my eyes on Jesus, who will do what He tells me He will do.

I don't want to keep my eyes on people who can try to make me look bad.

I want to keep my eyes on Jesus, who makes me look good for doing His will.

I don't want to keep my eyes on people who can give me evil eye looks.

I want to keep my eyes on Jesus, who gives me His kind looks of mercy.

I don't want to keep my eyes on people who can ruin my reputation.

I want to keep my eyes on Jesus, who gives me a good reputation for loving Him and keeping His Commandments.

I don't want to keep my eyes on people who may not care anything about what I'm doing for the Lord.

I want to keep my eyes on Jesus, who always cares about what I am doing in His holy name.

I don't want to keep my eyes on people who can condemn me to Hell.

I want to keep my eyes on Jesus, who wants to save me from being lost in Hell.

I don't want to keep my eyes on people who can betray me.

I want to keep my eyes on Jesus, who will never betray me.

I don't want to keep my eyes on people who can laugh at me.

I want to keep my eyes on Jesus, who will never laugh at me.

I don't want to keep my eyes on people who can cause me to sin.

I want to keep my eyes on Jesus, who wants to cleanse me from my sins.

I don't want to keep my eyes on people who can twist their words up on me.

I want to keep my eyes on Jesus, who makes His words straight with me.

I don't want to keep my eyes on people who can confuse me.

I want to keep my eyes on Jesus, who will never confuse me.

I don't want to keep my eyes on people who can plot evil things against me.

I want to keep my eyes on Jesus, who is good to me all the time.

I don't want to keep my eyes on people who may not be true to me.

I want to keep my eyes on Jesus, who is always true to me.

I don't want to keep my eyes on people who may try to butter me up to do what they want me to do

I want to keep my eyes on Jesus, who will tell me like it is and let me choose to do what He wants me to do.

Actions

There are people who will do something good by their actions for the wrong reasons.

There are people who will do good deeds through their actions, just to draw attention to themselves.

Do actions always tell the truth?

Is killing someone a bad action if it's in self-defense?

There are people who go through the action of going to church, but their hearts are filled with ill feelings towards someone.

Their action of going to church can look so true but be so false because they have ill feelings towards someone whether they're in the church or outside the church.

Judas's actions looked so true before the other disciples of Jesus Christ, but Jesus knew that Judas's actions were false.

Jesus knew that Judas would betray him when the other disciples didn't know that.

Do actions always tell the truth?

Someone can do something good to try to make themselves look good so that people will talk nicely about them.

Many people do good things, but the reasons for their actions are false and selfish before the Lord.

The Lord always knows our true hearts and can see beyond our actions to know whether they are true or false.

Only the Lord can judge our actions.

He knows our motives and intentions and whether they are good or bad, even when our actions may fool other people.

Actions can never fool God, but actions can sometimes fool people.

Many people will do good things, but their actions won't give God the glory and praise.

Those actions look so worthless to God, even though they might look good to people.

Do actions always tell the truth?

When Jacob pretended to be his brother Esau so his father Isaac would bless him, Jacob's actions were not true.

God knew Isaac blessed Jacob, but Isaac believed that he had blessed Esau.

Someone can do something good for you and me with his or her actions, but they can want something in return for what they have done, which is selfish.

Many people will say you know people by their actions.

Do we always know people by their actions?

Some people will do good things and then boast about it to make their actions look even better.

People whose actions are true don't have to boast about them to bless others.

Someone can do something bad on the spur of the moment, and this action is not as bad as a bad action that is planned by someone.

There are spur-of-the-moment actions and there are planned actions.

If you mistakenly do something bad, it is not as serious as planning to do something bad.

If we do something good for the wrong reasons, then our actions are not true.

Only the Lord will always know if our actions are true or false.

Good Men and Good Women

There are many wicked men and women who are so much smarter than me.

Many of them are in high positions and rule over me every day.

Many of them are rich and look down on me as if I am trash that needs to be put in the dumpster.

There are many wicked men and women I have to live among, and I hope that they won't set traps for me to fall into.

I know that the wicked will always be around me every day, but no wicked person can stop me from making Jesus Christ my choice each day.

Good men and good women are a blessing to me every day.

I love living my life among good men and good women, whether they believe in Jesus Christ or don't believe in Jesus Christ.

I truly thank the Lord for many good men and good women who are so much smarter than I am.

I know that good men and good women who are much smarter than me won't try to make me look stupid if I say something they don't agree with.

Good men and good women won't try to make me look like I don't know what I'm talking about.

Good men and good women may misunderstand me, but they won't try to make me feel small if I am not on their educational level.

Good men and good women can be hard to come by, even in the church.

The church seems to have a few good Christian men and women who don't act like they know it all.

Good men and good women are from the Lord, no matter the color of their skin.

Good men and good women are from the Lord, no matter what church they go to.

Good men and good women are from the Lord, no matter if they are rich or poor.

Good men and good women are from the Lord, no matter if they are educated or not educated.

The Lord's favor is upon good men and good women who are not perfect but are surely a blessing to be around and talk to.

Good men and good women are easy to love because good men and good women are loving people who do not believe that they are better than you and me.

If People Can't Control You and Me

If people can't control you and me and make us do what they want us to do, then they don't like us.

If people can't control you and me and make us do what they want us to do, then they don't want to talk to us.

If people can't control you and me and make us do what they want us to do, then they don't want to be around us.

If people can't control you and me and make us do what they want us to do, then they will talk bad about us.

Some of those people can be our kinfolks who want to control us.

Some of those people can be our so-called friends who want to control us.

Some of those people can be church folks who want to control you and me.

If people can't control you and me and make us do what they want us to do, then they will hold a grudge against us.

Controlling people are very selfish people who are only interested in themselves.

Controlling people don't want to admit their wrongdoings.

Controlling people don't see that they need to change.

Controlling people will only see what they believe to be right in their own eyes.

Controlling people are very proud about being in charge of others.

Controlling people don't see anything wrong about what they say.

Controlling people won't let you and me forget that we are wrong and they are right about what they want us to do.

Some people will fight us if they can't control us.

Some people will hurt us if they can't control us.

Some people hate us if they can't control us.

Some people will kill us if they can't control us.

If people can't control you and me, then they might very well become our enemies.

The good Lord Jesus Christ will never control you and me and make us do what He wants us to do.

The Lord will never control you and me and try to make us love and obey Him.

The Lord has given us free will so we can make our own choices.

Controlling people don't love you and me, they only love being in control of us.

There is Nothing Like Love

There is nothing like love that can make us feel so good.

There is nothing like love that can lift us up when we are feeling down.

There is nothing like love that can make us feel like we are on cloud nine.

There is nothing like love that can cause a bad person to want to be good.

There is nothing like love that can give us a good outlook on life.

There is nothing like love that can make us strong when we are weak.

There is nothing like love that can cause a war to end.

There is nothing like love that can cause an enemy to become a friend.

There is nothing like love that can cause us to forgive those who do us wrong.

There is nothing like love that can cause us to go the extra mile.

There is nothing like love that can cause us to give a helping hand.

There is nothing like love that will warn us of trouble.

There is nothing like love that can cause us to keep peace with our enemies.

There is nothing like love that will give us justice.

There is nothing like love that will not discriminate.

There is nothing like love that is not judgmental.

There is nothing like love that is very protective over our lives.

There is nothing like love that doesn't forget our birthdays.

There is nothing like love that doesn't forget our anniversaries.

There is nothing like love that tells us the truth.

There is nothing like love that won't pretend with us.

There is nothing like love that won't try to control us.

There is nothing like love that won't gossip about us.

There is nothing like love that won't change on us.

There is nothing like love that shows no favoritism.

There is nothing like love that won't put us down.

There is nothing like love that won't look down on us.

There is nothing like the love of God.

There is nothing like the love of Jesus Christ, who gave up His life on the cross for our sins.

There is nothing like love that is the Holy Spirit revealing all truth to us.

There is nothing like love that won't be jealous of us.

There is nothing like love that is not prejudiced against us.

There is nothing like love that won't use us.

There is nothing like love that will not break our hearts.

There is nothing like love that won't hate us.

There is nothing like love that will appreciate us.

There is nothing like love that will treat us right.

There is nothing like love that will talk to us right.

There is nothing like love that won't abandon us.

There is nothing like love that won't tell us a lie.

There is nothing like love that won't trick us.

There is nothing like love that is patient with us.

There is nothing like love that won't give up on us.

There is nothing like love that will support us.

There is nothing like love that will rejoice with us.

There is nothing like love that will stick by our side.

There is nothing like love that will smile at us.

There is nothing like love that says thank you.

There is nothing like love that accepts us for who we are.

There's nothing like love that gives us good advice.

There is nothing like love that will do good for us every day.

There is nothing like love that will finish the good things it starts.

There is nothing like love that no sickness can cause to run away.

There is nothing like love that no death can cause to deteriorate.

There is nothing like love that will take a chance.

There is nothing like love that will give us its full attention.

There is nothing like love that will listen to us.

There is nothing like love that will not deceive us.

There is nothing like love that is everlasting in God.

There is nothing like God's love, who so loved us first.

How Can Our Hearts Be Right with the Lord?

How can our hearts be right with the Lord if our hearts are not right with all of our brothers and sisters in the Lord?

Our hearts can't be right with the Lord if we are holding ill feelings towards others.

If we believe that our hearts can be right with some people and not right with some other people then we are showing respect of persons.

It's easy to love those who love you and me, whose heart is right with those who love us.

The Lord tells us to also love our enemies, who we might also have in the church.

Even though our enemies don't love us, we have no good excuse to not love them when we were all enemies of God and didn't know it.

So how can our hearts be right with the Lord Jesus Christ if we don't mean all of our brothers and sisters good and well, even if some of them don't mean us good and well?

Only the Lord truly knows what people are going through in their lives from day to day.

Only the Lord truly knows people's weaknesses from day today.

Only the Lord truly knows that everyone is struggling with some problems in their lives.

Every Christian should know better and give their problems to the Lord.

Every Christian should know better and love everyone inside the church and outside the church, regardless of whether things always go their way.

Everything will not go our way with all of our brothers and sisters in the Lord.

You and I have no right to hold grudges against people and take them off of our love list when this happens.

Jesus Christ, our Lord, doesn't always get His holy way with you and me.

When this happens, He doesn't hold that against us, even though we would be better off never having been born if He did hold it against us.

You and I can't manipulate the Lord into taking anyone off of His love list just because we have taken them off of our love list because we can't get our way with them.

We can sometimes try to make it seem like our way of doing things is God's way of doing things when dealing with people we approve or disapprove of.

How can our hearts be right with the Lord if we pick and choose who we should love or not love?

The biggest problem we can have is that our hearts are not right with ourselves, and therefore cannot be right with the Lord.

We can be good pretenders and even make many people in the church believe that our hearts are right with the Lord.

You and I can never pretend with the Lord.

The Lord is so loving and suffers along with us to help us get our hearts right with Him so that we can get our hearts right with one another.

There will be no ill feelings toward people and no holding grudges in heaven.

If we truly love God, we will truly love everybody inside the church and outside the church.

How are we to believe that we know what love is if we don't truly love God?

You and I can believe that our hearts are right with the Lord Jesus Christ, but if our hearts are not right with one another then how can our hearts be right with the Lord?

The Beginning

The beginning was here before we were born.

Our lives began in our mothers' wombs, forevermore after the beginning.

The beginning was here before the heavens and earth that the beginning created.

The beginning was here before the universe existed.

The beginning was here before other worlds.

The beginning is the source of life.

No one knows how the beginning began.

The beginning didn't begin with a big bang.

The beginning was here before any kind of theory.

The beginning is God.

The beginning was the word of God.

The beginning was made flesh in the image of God.

The beginning spoke to prophets.

The beginning was here before the angels.

The beginning created the angels.

The beginning created a man and woman.

The beginning created all the animals.

The beginning created the sun, moon and stars.

The beginning created all things in heaven and on earth.

The beginning was here before all things.

You and I began in our mothers' wombs.

The beginning began with God.

No one knows how God began.

No one knows when God began.

We can believe that life began with God and not with a big bang in the outer space.

No one knows where God began.

The beginning is forevermore beyond our imagination.

The beginning is forevermore beyond our knowledge.

The beginning is forevermore beyond science and technology.

The beginning is forevermore beyond our wisdom.

No man or woman was there in the beginning.

No angel was there in the beginning.

Only God was there in the beginning, which was God.

The beginning is eternal.

The beginning is all-powerful.

The beginning is everlasting life.

The beginning is eternal glory.

The beginning is everlasting love.

The beginning is God the Father, God the Son and God the Holy Spirit.

They were there in the beginning and we will never understand that because our minds are fallible to the beginning.

The beginning is forevermore real beyond luck.

The beginning is forevermore real beyond any mystery.

The beginning is forevermore real beyond any phenomenon.

The beginning is God and Jesus Christ and the Holy Spirit.

No one can explain their existence in the beginning.

It's like trying to read and explain all the published books in the world.

It's like trying to explain what everyone is feeling in their hearts.

It's like trying to read and explain what is in everyone's minds.

We know that only God can do that.

No prophecy can explain the beginning that existed before any prophecy.

The beginning is God, and no one can question how God began.

We don't usually think about how water began, we just love to drink it to quench our thirst.

We don't usually think about how food began, we just love to eat food when we are hungry.

It's the same way with God.

We don't need to know how God began, but we can truly love God and be thankful that God can quench our thirsty souls and satisfy our hungry souls every day.

The beginning is God, who is also the end, and will put an end to death.

God will do that in the end to create a new earth.

In the beginning was God and not evolution or chance.

God was here for billions and billions of years.

God is the beginning of all life in heaven and on earth.

God is the beginning of all life in the universe.

God's end is eternal life.

In the beginning was God and not theories and science.

In the beginning was God and not an educated guess.

In the beginning was God and not creation.

In the beginning was God and no man knows how God began.

Who can reason that God began from evolution?

No man's reason can go back to the beginning and figure out God's existence.

No man's theories and imagination can erase God, who is the origin of life.

In the beginning was God, who is also the origin of love.

In the beginning was God, whose end is infinite when our end is short here on earth.

God's end is endless forevermore beyond all the stars that look so endless in the universe.

The beginning was God and is God forevermore beyond the beginning of a baby born into this world.

A Mystery

We all would love to solve a mystery — that will surely get our attention.

We all are drawn to a mystery.

A mystery excites our minds.

A mystery can take our minds to heights of uncertainty.

A mystery can keep our minds on guard to the unknown.

A mystery has a story that we don't know about.

A mystery is something that has already happened and we just don't know how it ends.

A mystery can puzzle our minds.

All through the night, the full white moonlight can shine so mysteriously with its glow.

In the night, a shooting star can look so mysterious as it moves across the sky and disappears.

The sun can set, and look so mysterious as it seems to go down into the deep ocean waters.

A mystery didn't create its own presence.

There is something much more profound than a mystery.

There is a mysterious God who has revealed some of His mysteries to us in His holy word.

God is the greatest mystery known to all of mankind, who doesn't know where God came from.

All we know is that God is God, who existed before all things.

We believe that there is a heaven, which is also like a mystery.

We believe that we will go there one day because we believe in His Son, Jesus Christ.

Jesus Christ revealed the mystery of God because Jesus is God to be one with God and the Holy Spirit.

They are the greatest mystery that no angel and no human being can ever solve.

Lucifer tried to solve the greatest mystery when he rebelled against heaven.

The Lord is forevermore profound above the most genius mind that doesn't even know the smallest mysteries of God's eternal existence.

If the angels don't know all of God's mysteries, then there is no way for us to ever know.

God created mysteries all around us, even in some of our dreams.

We can fail to solve the smallest mystery that is so plain and simple to God.

Only God can solve all mysteries.

Passing Through

We Christians are passing through the wilderness of time that is only present under the sun and will one day run out.

Every child of God is passing through the tunnels of no turning back to living in darkness.

We Christians are passing through the dark nights of troubled times that Jesus will one day light up with His peace when you and I see Him on the clouds of glory.

Jesus will pass you and me through the valley of death when we one day receive our immortal bodies so we can live with Him forever and ever.

We Christians are passing through this sinful world of lies and deception that God's holy word shatters into pieces that no rebellious person can put back together.

We Christians are passing through hearts that wax cold, but Jesus will keep our hearts and minds warm in His love every day.

Jesus has given us Christians His protection so we can pass through our unhealthy lifestyles.

We Christians are passing through this dead-end world that has no highway to heaven.

Jesus Christ is the highway to heaven every day.

We Christians must hold onto Jesus, who has passed through this sinful world and gone back to heaven with the victory over our sins and death.

We Christians must not hold onto this world, because it is temporary and will one day pass away.

Anyone here on earth can choose to believe in Jesus Christ and become a Christian so they can pass through false doctrines and wolves in sheep's clothing.

We Christians are passing through this sinful world and avoiding the devil and all of his followers.

We Christians are passing through this world's technology that is like trash in the trash can compared to God's technology in heaven and other worlds.

We Christians are passing through science in this sinful world where science is not all truth to set us free from the devil's lies.

Only Jesus Christ is all truth, because he is the living truth that will set us free from all of the devil's lies that are against God's holy word every day.

Every day, we Christians are passing through minds that are not focused on Jesus, who will renew our minds every day if we keep our thoughts on Him.

This World

This world will get worse and worse in disobedience against God.

This world will get more and more liars.

This world will get more and more murderers.

This world will get more and more thieves.

This world will get more and more adulterers.

This world will get more and more fornicaters.

This world will get worse and worse.

This world will get more and more viruses.

This world will get more and more diseases.

This world will get more and more hurricanes.

This world will get more and more tornadoes.
This world will get worse and worse.

This world will get more and more injustice.

This world will get more and more riots.

This world will get more and more same-sex marriages.

This world will get more and more violent.

This world will get more and more broken-hearted people.

This world will get worse and worse.

This world will get more and more floods.

This world will get more and more selfish people.

This world will get more and more hypocrites.

This world will get more and more deceiving people.

This world will get more and more poor people.

This world will get more and more rich people.

This world will get more and more depressed people.

This world will get more and more mentally ill people.

This world will get worse and worse.

This world will get more and more babies being born out of wedlock.

This world will get more and more children being sexually assaulted.

This world will get more and more women being sexually assaulted.

This world will get more and more workaholics.

This world will get more and more people being out of work.

This world will get more and more wildfires.

This world will get more and more greedy people.

This world will get more and more overweight people.

This world will get more and more proud people.

This world will get more and more immoral people.

This world will get more and more people who don't believe in Jesus Christ.

This world will get more and more people who will stay away from the Lord.

This world will get more and more sex trafficking.

This world will get worse and worse before Jesus Christ comes back again.

This world will get more and more religious false doctrines.

This world will get more and more religious fanatics.

This world will get more and more pretenders, even in the church.

This world will get more and more evil people.

This world will get more and more unfaithful people.

This world will get more and more untrustworthy people.

This world will get worse and worse.

This world will get more and more people living in their sins.

This world will get more and more crooked people.

This world will get more and more heatwaves.

This world will get more and more storms.

This world will get more and more unforgiving people.

This world will get more and more sick people

This world will get more and more judgmental people.

This world will get worse and worse in these last days.

This world will get more and more prejudiced people.

This world will get more and more atheists.

This world will get more and more obsessed people.

This world will get more and more discontent people.

This world will get worse and worse in rebellion against God.

This world will get more and more people being lost in their sins.

This world will get more and more people being lovers of themselves.

This world will get more and more people divorcing their spouses.

This world will get more and more people who love to gossip.

This world will get more and more bad news on TV.

This world will get more and more revengeful people.

This world will get more and more hard-hearted people.

This world will get more and more controlling people.

This world will get worse and worse, just like the Bible says.

This world will get more and more hasty people.

This world will get more and more jealous people.

This world will get more and more wars.

This world will get more and more inequality.

This world will get more and more bad policemen.

This world will get more and more criminals.

This world will get more and more backbiting people.

This world will get worse and worse, but Jesus Christ, our Lord, will save you and me from being lost if we love and obey Him every day.

This world will get more and more unrealistic people.

This world will get more and more troublesome people.

This world will get more and more rude people.

This world will get more and more crazy people.

This world will get more and more road-ragers.

This world will get more and more disrespectful people.

This world will get more and more fearful people.

This world will get worse and worse before it comes to an end.

This world will get more and more unsafe to live in.

This world will get more and more unpredictable people.

This world will get more and more unstable people.

This world will get more and more foolish people.

This world will get more and more intelligent evil people.

This world will get more and more brilliant evil people.

This world will get more and more genius evil people.

This world will get more and more materialistic people.

This world will get worse and worse, but Jesus Christ will keep His promise to you and me for denying ourselves and picking up our crosses to follow Him every day.

This world will get more and more people believing that they can talk to the dead.

This world will get more and more deaths.

This world will get more and more people speaking profanity.

This world will get more and more idol worshippers.

This world will get more and more people singing songs about the creature who can't save them from their sins.

This world will get more and more homeless people.

This world will get more and more animal abusers.

This world will get more and more starvation.

This world will get more and more lazy people.

This world will get more and more filthy people.

This world will get more and more out of control people.

This world will get more and more insecure people.

This world will get more and more codependent people.

This world will get more and more seductive people.

This world will get worse and worse, with many people turning away from God.

This world will get more and more corrupt government leaders.

This world will get more and more lip service people.

This world will get more and more disobedient children.

This world will get more and more people wanting what belongs to someone else.

This world will get worse and worse, with many people breaking God's Ten Commandments.

This world will get more and more drug addicts.

This world will get more and more alcoholics.

This world will get more and more sex addicts.

This world will get more and more people who live for drama.

This world will get more and more angry people.

This world will get more and more hateful people.

This world will get more and more unhealthy people.

This world will get worse and worse, with many people denying the Lord Jesus Christ.

This world will get more and more people who will hear the truth of God's word and reject it.

This world will get more and more people making excuses for their sins.

This world will get more and more people not confessing and repenting of their sins unto the Lord Jesus Christ.

This world will get worse and worse, but Jesus Christ will seal you and me so that we can go with Him back to heaven if we love and obey Him in this sinful world that so many people make their home.

This world will get more and more people playing church.

This world will get more and more people playing God.

This world will get more and more people not believing that Jesus Christ is coming back again.

This world will get worse and worse and time is running out.

This world will get more and more mass shootings.

This world will get more and more protests.

This world will get more and more educated fools.

This world will get more and more feeble-minded people.

This world will get more and more people who worship the human body.

This world will get more and more people wanting to be praised.

This world will get more and more people pleasing man rather than pleasing God.

This world will get more and more people being falsely accused of doing something that they didn't do.

This world will get more and more people believing that they're better than you and me.

This world will get more and more people believing that Jesus Christ is worthless to them.

This world will get worse and worse, because so many people love confrontation.

This world will get more and more people showing respect of persons.

This world will get more and more people doubting what the Lord can do for them.

This world will get more and more bad laws from immoral politicians.

This world will get worse and worse, but God will write our names in His book of life if we hold on to Jesus like it's our last day to live.

This world will get more and more children getting abused.

This world will get more and more women getting abused.

This world will get more and more transgender people.

This world will get worse and worse as time goes on.

This world will get more and more serial killers.

This world will get more and more hostile people.

This world will get more and more people committing fraud.

This world will get more and more nuclear weapons.

This world will get more and more fault-finding people.

This world will get more and more cyber attacks.

This world will get more and more home intrusions.

This world will get worse and worse by the second, minute and hour, but Jesus Christ has already given you and me the victory to overcome this world's distress.

This world will get more and more women getting abortions.

This world will get more and more fatherless children.

This world will get more and more disabled people.

This world will get more and more health professionals getting sued for malpractice.

This world will get more and more people being victims of theft.

This world will get more and more people getting food poisoning.
This world will get more and more people neglecting their children.

This world will get more and more people cheating on their spouses.

This world will get more and more single men and single women living together without being married.

This world will get worse and worse, but Jesus Christ can save men, women, boys and girls.

This world will get more and more people making bad choices.

This world will get more and more people believing in witchcraft.

This world will get more and more people believing in horoscopes.

This world will get more and more people believing in luck.

This world will get more and more people believing in magic.

This world will get worse and worse, but Jesus Christ will save you and me because we believe in Him, who is forever more powerful than witchcraft, horoscopes, luck and magic.

This world will get more and more people believing in evolution.

This world will get worse and worse, but Jesus Christ is the living truth beyond chance.

This world will get more and more people committing suicide.

This world will get more and more high-minded people.

This world will get more and more people living in pleasure.

This world will get more and more people who can't be trusted.

This world will get more and more people getting instant fame.

This world will get more and more people being spies for other nations.

This world will get more and more people ruining someone's good name.

This world will get more and more people taking illegal drugs.

This world will get more and more people getting into accidents.

This world will get more and more people going to court.

This world will get worse and worse, but Jesus Christ will represent you and me in the courtroom of heaven if we live our lives to represent Him in this world.

This world will get more and more people getting put in prison.

This world will get more and more people joking about serious problems.

This world will get more and more people not taking good care of themselves.

This world will get more and more people buying things that they don't need.

This world will get more and more people not waiting on the Lord to work things out for them.

This world will get worse and worse, but the Lord Jesus Christ will supply all of our needs if we wait on Him who is always on time.

This world will get more and more people having bad motives.

This world will get more and more people having bad intentions.

This world will get more and more people believing a lie to be the truth.

This world will get more and more church folks loving their pastor more than they love Jesus.

This world will get more and more church folks who will not read the Bible.

This world will get more and more church folks misinterpreting the Bible.

This world will get more and more church folks believing they don't have to keep God's Commandments.

This world will get more and more church folks dressing like the people of the world.

This world will get more and more church folks acting like the people of the world.

This world will get more and more church folks causing people to leave the church.

This world will get more and more church folks pretending to be Christian.

This world will get more and more Christian folks not giving up things that displease the Lord Jesus Christ.

This world will get worse and worse, and many will be called but only a few will choose to give all of their hearts to the Lord Jesus Christ.

This world will get more and more people planning to do evil things.

This world will get more and more people running into trouble.

This world will get more and more people not believing the truth.

This world will get more and more people not wanting to hear the truth.

This world will get more and more people keeping silent about injustice.

This world will get more and more people praying to idols.

This world will get more and more people crushing someone's dreams.

This world will get worse and worse, but Jesus Christ is forever more real than any dream and He will be faithful and true to you and me.

This world will get more and more conniving people.

This world will get more and more mean people.

This world will get more and more people having a superior attitude.

This world will get worse and worse, but Jesus Christ is superior over all the angels in heaven as well as being superior over this world and over the fallen angels.

This world will get more and more people putting trust in their mental powers that are no match for the Lord Jesus Christ, who is all-powerful.

This world will get more and more people putting trust in their physical strength that can go flat like a tire if the Lord commands it to.

This world will get worse and worse, but Jesus Christ is forevermore stronger than Samson was and He will fight our battles and always win just by speaking the word that can calm the strongest storms.

True Freedom

Many people from oppressed nations would love to live in a nation where they can be free and prosper.

Many people will feel so good about becoming a citizen of a prosperous nation.

They will have the freedom to get an education.

They will have the freedom to start their own business.

They will have the freedom to travel throughout the nation.

They will have freedom of speech.

They will have the freedom to vote.

Many oppressed people from other nations dream about coming to a nation where they can escape oppression.

They want to be freed from the fear of their lives being in danger

They want to be freed from living in poverty.

They want to be freed from a corrupt government pressing them down with unlawful practices.

No one in their right mind would love to live in a corrupt nation.

Many oppressed people love to come to a nation where they can be free from oppression.

Any good and normal person wants to live in a nation where they are safe.

Even a corrupt person wants to be free to do more and more bad things.

True freedom is to believe in the Lord Jesus Christ.

True freedom is to have hope in the Lord.

True freedom is to love the Lord.

True freedom is to obey the Lord's Ten Commandments.

True freedom is to be saved in the Lord Jesus Christ.

We can live in a nation where we have so much freedom but still we are in the bondage of sin.

We are only truly free in Jesus Christ, who is the truth to set us free from living in darkness that has no freedom for you and me.

Sin is oppression in every nation that needs the Lord's guidance every day.

A nation can only be free in the Lord, who gives you and me true freedom for having faith in Him.

Use Your

Use your voice for good. Don't use your voice for evil.

Use your hearing for good. Don't use your hearing for evil.

Use your eyesight for good. Don't use your eyesight for evil.

Use your hands for good. Don't use your hands for evil.

Use your feet for good. Don't use your feet for evil.

Use your thoughts for good. Don't use your thoughts for evil.

Use your imagination for good. Don't use your imagination for evil.

Use your mind for good. Don't use your mind for evil.

Use your feelings for good. Don't use your feelings for evil.

Use your emotions for good. Don't use your emotions for evil.

Use your heart for good. Don't use your heart evil.

Use your talents for good. Don't use your talents for evil.

Use your skills for good. Don't use your skills for evil.

Use your laughs for good. Don't use your laughs for evil.

Use your intelligence for good. Don't use your intelligence for evil.

Use your education for good. Don't use your education for evil.

Use your wealth for good. Don't use your wealth for evil.

Use your time for good. Don't use your time for evil.

Use your actions for good. Don't use your actions for evil.

Use your life for good. Don't use your life for evil.

Use your choices for good. Don't use your choices for evil.

When Jesus Christ lived on earth, He was good all the time.

It was a good thing when Jesus called the Pharisees and scribes hypocrites.

It was a good thing when Jesus turned over the tables of the moneychangers in His holy temple.

When Jesus lived here on earth, He did everything good.

Use your smiles for good. Don't use your smiles for evil.

Use your habits for good. Don't use your habits for evil.

Use your motives for good. Don't use your motives for evil.

Use your intentions for good. Don't use your intentions for evil.

Use your existence for good. Don't use your existence for evil.

Use your common sense for good. Don't use your common sense for evil.

Use your genius for good. Don't use your genius for evil.

Of Their Own Race

Many people are killing people of their own race.

Many people are stealing from people of their own race.

Many people are deceiving people of their own race.

Many people are lying to people of their own race.

Many people are jealous of people of their own race.

Many people are violent to people of their own race.

Many people are using people of their own race.

Many people are manipulating people of their own race.

Many people are fighting people of their own race.

Many people are quarreling with people of their own race.

Many people are not helping people of their own race.

Many people are afraid of people of their own race.

Many people don't trust people of their own race.

Many people don't love people of their own race.

Many people gossip about people of their own race.

Many people talk badly about people of their own race.

Many people treat people of their own race badly.

Many people will disrespect people of their own race.

Many people will put down people of their own race.

Many people will joke about people of their own race.

Many people will despise people of their own race.

Many people disown people of their own race.

Many people laugh at people of their own race.

Many people judge people of their own race.

Many people pull down people of their own race.

There is no perfect race of people in this sinful world.

Jesus Christ gave up His life to save every race of people from their sins.

In the beginning, there was only one race of people and one language in this world.

God, Himself, caused mankind to speak different languages because of man's rebellion against Him.

The different languages became different races of people.

There was one race and one language of people who tried to build a tower because they wanted to reach way up in the sky above the highest mountaintop.

Today there are many different races that use many different languages all around this world.

Every race of people has many problems that only Jesus Christ can solve.

Jesus solved those problems when He rose from the grave with victory over all sins.

We will always have problems in our own race of people until Jesus comes back again.

Only Jesus can restore us back to one race of people with one language in the new heaven and new earth.

Just imagine when Jesus comes back again, He will give us an immortal body and we will hopefully be one color of people with one language and we will all be happy to see and give Jesus all the praise and glory.

Many people are causing the people of their own race to be lost in their sins.

Many people deny the problems in their own race.

Many people won't talk about the problems in their own race.

Many people cover up the problems in their own race.

Many people reject people in their own race.

Many people show favoritism to their own race.

Many people don't want to have anything to do with people of their own race.

It is hard when one race of people hates another race of people.

It is hard when one race of people oppresses another race of people.

It is much harder when people oppress their own race with abuse, violence, drugs, jealousy, manipulations, disrespect and murderers.

Sin has affected every race of people who speak every language, making them treat people of their own race badly.

No race of people has the excuse to believe that they can't tell what is right and good, because God put His law in everybody's hearts so that they can tell the difference between right and wrong and good and bad.

God created us all in His own image so that we could reason things through with good sense.

Animals can't choose to do right from wrong.

There is No Good Life In

There is no good life in telling lies.

There is no good life in using people.

There is no good life in getting revenge.

There is no good life in treating people badly.

There is no good life in talking bad about people.

There is no good life in killing people.
There is no good life in stealing.

There is no good life in cheating people.

There is no good life in being greedy for worldly gain.

There is no good life in fornicating.

There is no good life in living in adultery.

There is no good life in being prejudiced.

There is no good life in deceiving people.

There is no good life in fooling people.

There is no good life in showing respect of persons.

There is no good life in not loving all of your brothers and sisters in the Lord.

There is no good life in disunity.

There is no good life in cliques.

There is no good life in not obeying your parents.

There is no good life in being lazy.

There is no good life in not helping others.

There is no good life in believing that you are better than others.

There is no good life in doing evil things.

There is no good life in being discontent.

There is no good life in not taking good care of yourself.

There is no good life in not taking good care of your children.

There is no good life in not taking good care of your pets.

There is no good life in not keeping your word.

There is no good life in saying one thing and doing another thing.

There is no good life in teasing people.

There is no good life in bullying people.

There is no good life in manipulating people.

There is no good life in hurting people.

There is no good life in giving people injustice.

There is no good life in putting people down.

There is no good life in division.

There is no good life in wars.

There is no good life in being jealous of people.

There is no good life in despising people.

There is no good life in making trouble for people.

There is no good life in not forgiving people.

There is no good life in trying to control people.

There is no good life in not loving your neighbors.

There is no good life in not believing in Jesus Christ.

There is no good life in rejecting Jesus Christ.

There is no good life in not loving Jesus Christ.

There is no good life in turning your back on Jesus Christ.

There is no good life in not being saved in Jesus Christ.

There is no good life without Jesus Christ being in your life.

There is no good life in living in sin.

The devil can be really good at causing many people to believe that living in this sinful world is the good life.

The devil has caused many people to believe that the good life is doing your own will.

The devil has caused many people to believe that the good life is speaking your own words and doing your own thing.

The good life is doing God's holy will.

The good life is loving God and keeping His commandments.

There is no good life in disobeying the Lord Jesus Christ.

There is no good life in loving the creature more than loving God.

There is no good life in loving material things more than loving God.

There is no good life in loving temporary things more than loving God, who is eternal.

There is no good life in not confessing and repenting of your sins unto the Lord Jesus Christ.

There is no good life in playing church.

There is no good life in playing god.

There is no good life in pretense.

There is no good life in pride and arrogance.

There is no good life in being away from God.

Many people believe

Many people believe they can break rules and regulations and get away with it.

Some people get away with breaking some rules and regulations.

Many people believe they can break the laws of the land and get away with it.

Some people do break some laws of the land and get away with it.

Some people act like they are above the law and they break it.

Many people believe that no one cares if they break rules and regulations.

Many people believe that no one cares if they break the law.

Many people don't care if they break the laws of the land.

Many people believe that no one will ever know if they break rules and regulations.

Many people believe that no one will ever know if they break the laws of the land.

Many people break rules and regulations like it's nothing bad to do.

Many people break the laws of the land like it's nothing bad to do.

Many people believe that they can break rules, and regulations, and they feel good about breaking them.

Many people believe that they can break the laws of the land, and they feel good about breaking the laws.

Many people will break rules and regulations, and make excuses for breaking them.

Many people will break the laws of the land, and make excuses for breaking them.

Many people will break rules and regulations, and won't admit that they broke them.

Many people will break the laws of the land, and won't admit that they broke the law.

Many people believe that they can break God's Ten Commandments, and God will let them get away with breaking His holy law.

Many people believe that they can break God's Ten Commandments and God will overlook it.

Many church folks believe that they can break God's Ten Commandments and still be saved in Jesus Christ.

Many people believe that they can break God's Ten Commandments and go to heaven, but Jesus says, "If you love Me you will keep My commandments."

Many people believe that they can love Jesus and not keep His Commandments that every true Christian won't willfully break.

Will Use Jesus's Name

Many people will use Jesus's name like it's worthless.

Many people will use Jesus's name like it's a joke.

Many people will use Jesus's name like it's unrealistic.

Many people will use Jesus's name like it has no power.

Many people will use Jesus's name like it's useless.

Many people will use Jesus's name like it's a fraud.

Many people will use Jesus's name like it's a lie.

Many people will use Jesus's name like it's a fake.

Many people will use Jesus's name like it's dead.

Many people will use Jesus's name like it's not holy.

Many people will use Jesus's name like it's not righteous.

Many people will use Jesus's name like it's not perfect.

Many people will use Jesus's name like it means nothing.

Many people will use Jesus's name like it's bad.

Many people will use Jesus's name in a reckless way.

Many people will use Jesus's name in a careless way.

Many people will use Jesus's name like it's bondage.

Many people will use Jesus's name like it's a scam.

Many people will use Jesus's name like playing the lottery.

Many people will use Jesus's name like it's broken glass.

Many people will use Jesus's name like it's garbage.

Many people will use Jesus's name like it's a dry well.

Many people will use Jesus's name like it's a bad storm.

Many people will use Jesus's name like it's untrustworthy.

Many people will use Jesus's name like it's deceitful.

Many people will use Jesus's name like it's a game to play.

Many people don't believe in Jesus Christ, and will use His name like it's a fairy tale.

Many people don't believe in Jesus Christ, and will use His name like it's sinful.

Many people don't believe in Jesus Christ, and will use His name like it's a waste of their time.

Many people will use Jesus's name like it's a get rich gimmick.

Many people will use Jesus's name any old kind of way.

Many people will use Jesus's name like it's cheap.

Many people will use Jesus's name like it's not victorious.

Many people will use Jesus's name like it's funny.

Many people will use Jesus's name like it's weak.

Many people will use Jesus's name like it's below them.

Many people will use Jesus's name like it's sad.

Many people will use Jesus's name like it should not exist.

Many people will use Jesus's name in the wrong way.

Many people will use Jesus's name like it's a one-night stand.

Many people will use Jesus's name to cover up their bad motives.

Many people will use Jesus's name like it's entertainment.

Many people don't believe in Jesus Christ, and will use His name like it's out of date.

Many people don't believe in Jesus Christ, and will use His name like it has expired.

Many people will use Jesus's name like it's a burden.

Many people will use Jesus's name like it's not divine.

Oh Lord, You Always Know

Oh Lord, You always know me better than I will ever know myself.

Oh Lord, You always know what is good and not good for me.

Oh Lord, You always know what I can bear and what I can't bear.

Oh Lord, You always know whose life to shorten and you always know whose life to prolong.

Oh Lord, You always know all that I don't know.

Oh Lord, You always know all who hate me.

Oh Lord, You always know all who love me.

Oh Lord, You always know who talks bad about me.

Oh Lord, You always know all of my thoughts.

Oh Lord, You always know what I will say before I say it.

Oh Lord, You always know what I will do before I do it.

Oh Lord, You always know what I will dream before I dream it.

Oh Lord, You always know what I will see before I see it.

Oh Lord, You always know what I will hear before I hear it.

Oh Lord, You always know what I will feel before I feel it.

Oh Lord, You always know everything that I do.

Oh Lord, You always know everything that I feel.

Oh Lord, You always know all of my mind.

Old Lord, You are you always know all of my heart.

Oh Lord, You always do all of my life.

Oh Lord, You always know what choices I will make.

Old Lord, You always know all the right things that I do.

Oh Lord, You always know all the wrong things that I do.

Oh Lord, You always know all of my sins.

Oh Lord, You always know all of my weaknesses.

Oh Lord, You always know what I know.

Oh Lord, You always know all of my sins.

Oh Lord, You always know all of my disappointments.

Oh Lord, You always know all of my sorrow.

Oh Lord, You always know my joy.

Oh Lord, You always know all of my pain.

Oh Lord, You always know my destiny.

Oh Lord, You always know me every day.

Oh Lord, You always know everybody's mind, heart and soul.

Oh Lord, You always know everybody's choices and whether they choose You or reject You.

It can make us feel good

Our good works can't save us from our sins, but they can make us feel good when we're doing them.

Giving people a kind look can make us feel good.

Saying good words to people can make us feel good.

Forgiving people can make us feel good.

Faith without works is dead.

We can say that we have faith in Jesus Christ, but if we are not doing anything good in Jesus's name, then our works are dead.

Treating people right can make us feel good.

Helping people can make us feel good.

Encouraging people can make us feel good.

Not tailgating people on the road can make us feel good.

Respecting people can make us feel good.

Not being prejudiced against people can make us feel good.

Our good works can't save us from our sins, but they can surely add more years to our lives.

Giving people good advice can make us feel good.

Being good to people can make us feel good.

Not using people can make us feel good.

Being fair to people can make us feel good.

Being honest with people can make us feel good.

Our good works can't save us from our sins, but our good works can lift us up if we are feeling down.

Praying for people can make us feel good.

Living right before people can make us feel good.

Not making trouble before people can make us feel good.

Not mocking people can make us feel good.

Doing good works should make us feel good because the good things that we do for others will come back to us.

Good works with good motives and good intentions will surely make us feel good without a doubt.

Not judging people can make us feel good.

There are people who do evil things and feel good about doing evil things.

That kind of feeling good is evil.

The Lord wants us to feel good for doing His holy will.

The Lord wants you and me to be happy Christians.

The Lord wants you and me to be happy about doing good works in His holy name.

Good works can't save you and me from being lost in our sins, but they can be real proof that you and I love the Lord and obey Him.

The good works done in His name can make us feel so good every day.

If We Don't Put Our Trust In The Lord

If we don't put our trust in the Lord, we will set ourselves up for a big disappointment.

If we don't put our trust in the Lord, we will sooner or later regret it.

If we don't put our trust in the Lord, it will catch up with us one day.

If we don't put our trust in the Lord, we will worry about things we have no control over.

If we don't put our trust in the Lord, we will worry about what tomorrow may bring us.

If we don't put our trust in the Lord, our plans for the future will fail.

If we don't put our trust in the Lord, we will sooner or later mess things up in our lives.

If we don't put our trust in the Lord, we won't know what to do when trouble comes our way.

If we don't put our trust in the Lord, we will be a bad influence on those who put their trust in the Lord.

If we don't put our trust in the Lord, we will walk on the devil's playground.

If we don't put our trust in the Lord, we will deceive ourselves.

If we don't put our trust in the Lord, we will pay the cost.

If we don't put our trust in the Lord, the day will come for us to see what a big mistake we have made.

If we don't put our trust in the Lord, it will sooner or later show and tell on us.

If we don't put our trust in the Lord, it will have a bad effect on our life.

If we don't put our trust in the Lord, we will shorten our own lives.

If we don't put our trust in the Lord, even a fool would know that we are not wise.

If we don't put our trust in the Lord, sooner or later we will have some serious doubts about why we even exist.

If we don't put our trust in the Lord, whatever we say is like a dry well.

If we don't put our trust in the Lord, whatever we do is like a water vapor that evaporates in the air.

If we don't put our trust in the Lord, we have truly fooled ourselves about who we can trust.

If we don't put our trust in the Lord, we will sooner or later make our beds in hell.

The Battle of Good Against Evil

The battle of good against evil is within me.

That battle goes on every day inside of me.

Just because I'm a Christian doesn't mean that everything will go well for me every day.

If the devil has me where he wants me to be, then there will be no battle going on within me.

If a Christian says that their life is good all the time, then they are not walking on the straight and narrow road that leads to the Lord Jesus Christ.

The battle of good against evil should be going on in every Christian's life.

The devil will try his best to tempt every Christian to sin against God.

The devil will come at you and me every day in some kind of evil way.

The devil already has many people in the chains and bondage of their sins.

He has them exactly where he wants them to be because there is no battle of good against evil going on within them.

All who believe in the Lord Jesus Christ will have that battle of good against evil going on inside of them every day.

The devil hates for you and me to believe in Jesus Christ.

I can't say that I am a Christian and pretend like I have it good all the time.

I can't say that I am a Christian and pretend like there is no battle of good against evil going on inside of me.

Even though that battle is going on in every true Christian's life, we can truly thank Jesus Christ who got the victory over evil so it won't overcome the world.

Because of Jesus Christ, you and I will overcome evil with the goodness of the Lord dwelling in us.

If you call yourself a Christian and want others to believe that you don't ever have any problems in your life, then you must be right where the devil wants you to be because you are deceiving others with this falsehood.

Every true child of God will go through some hard times in their life for Jesus' holy name's sake.

The battle against good and evil is a battle that every Christian will face if they have the Holy Spirit within them.

Everybody Needs God

Everybody needs God, but a lot of people don't believe in God.

A lot of people don't want to believe in God.

Everybody needs God, but a lot of people will blame God for their suffering and pain.

A lot of people will blame God for their failures.

Everybody needs God, but a lot of people have turned their backs on God.

A lot of people will mock God.

Everybody needs God, but a lot of people don't want to believe in God's Son, Jesus Christ.

A lot of people don't believe that Jesus Christ is the Son of God.

A lot of people will get angry at God for not answering their prayers.

A lot of people will curse at God for not answering their prayers.

Everybody needs God, but God doesn't need you and me.

God can do all things without you and me.

Everybody needs God, but a lot of people believe that God needs them to help Him win lost souls.

Everybody needs God, but a lot of people don't believe that God made them successful in life.

A lot of people believe that they made themselves successful in life.

Everybody needs God, but a lot of people don't believe that God gave his Son, Jesus Christ, all power and authority over all the angels and all the world.

Everybody needs God, but a lot of people will worship the creature who didn't create all things.

A lot of people will worship themselves like they are god.

Everybody needs God, but a lot of people will worship this world that is filled with imperfect people.

A lot of people believe that they are perfect and have no sins to confess and repent unto God.

Everybody needs God, but a lot of people don't realize that they need God.

A lot of people don't care to realize that they need God.

Everybody needs God, but a lot of people don't believe they need the Holy Spirit to lead and guide them to God through his Son, Jesus Christ.

Common People

It's mostly common people who have caused other people to get rich.

It's mostly common people who built this nation and made it great.

It's mostly common people who are in the military.

It's mostly common people who fight in wars.

It's mostly common people who are disrespected.

It's mostly common people who are employees on the job.

It's mostly common people who go out to vote.

It's mostly common people who elect people to high office.

It's mostly common people who commit crimes.

It's mostly common people who get killed.

It's mostly common people who have common sense.

It's mostly common people who go to church.

It's mostly common people who believe in Jesus Christ.

It was mostly common people who were in the large crowds following Jesus Christ.

It was mostly common people who Jesus Christ ministered to.

It was mostly common people who loved Jesus Christ when He lived on earth.

It was mostly common people who Jesus healed.

It was mostly common people who Jesus preached to when He lived on earth.

It was mostly common people who were Jesus's disciples when He was here on earth.

It's mostly common people who live in this world.

It's mostly common people who help their fellow man.

It's mostly common people who don't believe they are better than others.

It's mostly common people who take the coats off of their backs and give them to you and me.

It's mostly common people who treat you and me right.

It's mostly common people who are friendly.

It's mostly common people who are not stuck up.

It's mostly common people who are saved in Jesus Christ.

It's mostly common people who are content.

It's mostly common people who are not greedy for worldly gain.

It's mostly common people who accept you and me for who we are.

It's mostly common people who will join Jesus Christ in heaven when He comes back again.

It's mostly common people who are treated unfairly.

It's mostly common people who get overlooked.

It's mostly common people who are poor.

It's mostly common people who work hard.

It's mostly common people who fear the Lord God.

Don't Look Down on People

Don't look down on people who are not educated.

Don't look down on people who are ignorant.

Don't look down on people who are slow Learners.

Don't look down on people who are handicapped.

Don't look down on people who are mentally ill.

Don't look down on people who are foolish.

Don't look down on people who are stupid.

Don't look down on people who are poor.

Don't look down on people who are not living in a big beautiful house.

Don't look down on people who are not driving a beautiful, expensive car.

Don't look down on people who don't have a job.

Don't look down on people who don't have good hygiene.

Don't look down on people who have failures in their lives.

Don't look down on people who made a lot of mistakes.

Don't look down on people who are short.

Don't look down on people who are small.

Don't look down on people who are weak minded.

Don't look down on people who are not good-looking.

Don't look down on people who don't talk right.

Don't look down on people who don't live right.

Don't look down on people who change their mind.

Don't look down on people who have turned their backs on the Lord.

Don't look down on people who talk too much.

Don't look down on people who don't talk much.

Don't look down on people who are against you.

When Jesus Christ lived here on Earth, He never looked down on anyone, even though He had every right to look down on all sinners like you and me.

Jesus never believed that He was too good to save anyone from their sins, which are nothing but poverty to God.

The heavens cannot contain all of God's will that is in Jesus Christ.

The Devil Knows

The devil knows that if he can cause us to show respect of persons, then you and I are not like Jesus Christ, who loves everybody the same and shows no favoritism.

The devil knows that if he can cause us to tell lies, then you and I are not like Jesus Christ who is the truth that cannot ever lie.

The devil knows that if he can cause us to not forgive others, then you and I are not like Jesus Christ who forgives us of our sins if we confess and repent.

When Jesus hung on the cross, He said to his Heavenly Father God, "Forgive them for they do not know what they do."

The devil knows that if he can cause us to have bad motives behind the good things we are doing, then you and I are not like Jesus Christ who had nothing but good motives behind every good thing that He did when He lived on earth.

The devil knows that if he can cause us to judge people, then you and I are not like Jesus Christ who is worthy to judge everybody right now by all the words we say and all the things we do.

The devil knows that if he can cause us to be proud, then you and I are not like Jesus Christ who was always humble when He lived on earth.

Jesus even humbled himself unto death to save us from being lost in our sins.

The devil knows that if he can cause us to do our own will, then you and I are not like Jesus Christ who always did His Heavenly Father's will when He lived on earth.

The devil knows that if he can cause us to talk badly about people, treat them badly and look down on them, then we are not like Jesus Christ who came to this sinful world to save us, not condemn us in our sins.

Something Always Comes Up

Something always comes up, sooner or later, when we least expect it.

Something always comes up that can surprise you and me.

Something always comes up and that can be a disappointment for you and me.

We love for good things to come up in our lives, but when bad things come up it can surely affect us in bad ways.

We can get things repaired in our houses, and then something else can break.

We can get well after being sick but then we can get sick again.

Something will always come up in this world and we won't always know what will be coming next.

When bad things come up, it can get us down.

When bad things come up, it can make us angry.

When good things come up, it can make us feel good.

When good things come up, it can cheer us up.

When good things come up, it can cause us to do better in life.

Something will always come up, sooner or later, in our lives.

Something will always come up with the Lord, who talks to us all the time in His holy word to let us know the right way to live day after day.

Something will always come up with the Lord, who gives you and me His holy spirit for making Him our choice day after day.

Something will always come up with the Lord, who is good to you and me all the time as long as we confess and repent of our sins unto Him.

Something will always come up with the Lord, and it will be something good that helps us hold onto Him.

Something will always come up with the Lord to help us keep our eyes on Him.

Something will always come up with the Lord to help us keep our trust in Him.

Something will always come up with the Lord Jesus Christ, who is always busy saving our souls from being lost.

Something will always come up with the devil, but the Lord is always ahead of the devil.

Something will always come up with the devil, but the Lord won't let the devil tempt us more than what we can handle.

Something will always come up with the devil, but the Lord will work things out for you and me on His time that is always on time.

Something will always come up with the devil, but the Lord cannot fail us.

Something will always come up with the devil, but the Lord will give us the strength to keep going and not give up.

Something will always come up, sooner or later, but the Lord is always for us and not against us if we love Him with all of our minds, hearts, souls and strength.

First Impression Shouldn't Always Be Lasting Impressions

No one can smile all of the time.

No one can be happy all the time

No one can be cheerful all the time.

People who love to smile can have a bad day, and then they may not smile at anyone.

Someone who sees them for the first time and doesn't know that they love to smile a lot might believe that they never smile.

That may be their first impression and lasting impression, even though it's wrong and that person is just having a bad day that caused them to not smile.

An evil person can make a good first impression on someone who doesn't know them.

That evil person can pretend to be so good and kind that someone who doesn't know them won't realize they're actually a serial killer.

Many women have fallen prey to serial killers because their first impressions told them they were dealing with a good person, when that person actually wants to kill them.

First impressions shouldn't always be lasting impressions about anyone.

Cheerful people can grieve sometimes, and might not be in a friendly frame of mind towards you and me.

We can meet these people for the first time and believe that they are not friendly because they didn't show themselves as friendly when we met them.

That man or woman might actually be friendly and easy to talk to when they are not feeling grief.

There is no way for you and me to know this based upon our first impressions.

To make our first impression our lasting impression can be a mistake.

Only Jesus Christ can always make a first impression be a lasting impression, because He knows the heart behind the outward appearance that can sometimes be mistaken by imperfect people.

No one is perfect, and no one can always make a good first impression.

Many people have made their first impression the lasting impression about someone and have been deceived.

Some first impressions are true, but many times the first impression is not true and should not be the lasting impression you have about someone.

There are many wolves in sheep's clothing.

They can make a good first impression on you and me, and we may believe that they are good, when in fact they are wolves and predators who love to prey on the sheep.

Imaginary

Many people imagine they are superheroes.

Many people imagine there is a Superman, Superwoman, Super Boy and Super Girl.

Many people imagine they are superhuman and have extra strength.

Many people have good imaginations and write imaginary books that get published.

Some of those imaginary books make lots of sales and become bestsellers.

Imagining things can be very powerful.

Many people imagine they are in a perfect relationship with someone.

Many people imagine they are in a perfect marriage.

Many people imagine they live in a perfect world.

Many people imagine they are all-powerful.

Many people imagine they are perfect.

Many people imagine they are god.

Many people believe that the Bible is imaginary.

Many people believe that Jesus Christ is imaginary.

Many people believe that God is imaginary.

Many people imagine they can walk on water.

Many people imagine they can calm the storm.

Many people imagine they have super powers.

Many people imagine they can rule the world.

Many people believe that heaven is imaginary.

Many people believe that angels are imaginary.

Many people believe that the devil is imaginary.

When Jesus walked on water, that was real and not imaginary to His disciples.

When Jesus calmed the storm, that was real and not imaginary to His disciples.

When Jesus fed the hungry, that was real and not imaginary to His disciples.

When Jesus cast out demons, that was real and not imaginary to His disciples.

When Jesus opened the eyes of the blind, that was real and not imaginary to His disciples.

When Jesus died on the cross, that was real and not imaginary to His disciples.

When Jesus rose from the grave, that was real and not imaginary to His disciples.

Jesus Christ was real, not imaginary to His disciples.

Many people today believe that Jesus is imaginary.

Many people today believe that eternal life is imaginary.

No one believes that they are imaginary.

We all believe that we are real, whether we live a long life or a short life.

There is nothing imaginary about God the Father, the Son and the Holy Spirit who created Adam and Eve, who were real human beings.

This world is filled with real people, not imaginary people.

Many people imagine they can do nothing wrong.

Many people imagine they can do anything they want.

Many men imagine they can get any woman they want to be with.

Many women imagine they can get any man they want to be with.

Many little girls imagine their doll babies can talk to them.

Many people imagine they are rich, and there are real rich people in the world.

Many people imagine they are flying a plane, and there are people who really are flying planes.

No one is living in imaginary life, because the lives we live are real.

No one is living an imaginary life, because our bodies can feel real pain.

No one is living an imaginary life, because we can get sick and die.

Many people imagine that they can talk to their dead loved ones but they are actually talking to Fallen Angels who appear to be their dead loved ones.

Those fallen angels are demons talking to those who believe they are talking to the dead.

Death is not imaginary for those who have lost loved ones.

Many people imagine they will never get caught doing bad things.

Who in their right mind would trade their real life for an imaginary life that doesn't exist?

Many people imagine they are saved, but they don't believe in Jesus Christ.

Doing Your Holy Will, O Lord

Doing Your holy will, O Lord, is so good for my Soul.

Doing Your holy will, O Lord, is so glorious.

Doing Your holy will, O Lord, is so magnificent.

Doing Your holy will, O Lord, is so very rewarding.

Doing Your holy will, O Lord, is more beautiful than any woman in this world.

Doing Your holy will, O Lord, is victorious.

Doing Your holy will, O Lord, is so great to me.

Doing Your holy will, O Lord is so vibrant to me.

Doing Your holy will, O Lord is the best thing in my life.

Doing Your holy will, O Lord, gives me the strength to keep going on.

Doing Your holy will, O Lord, gives me peace of mind.

Doing Your holy will, O Lord, lifts me up on a spiritual high.

Doing Your holy will, O Lord, is every good thing to me.

Doing Your holy will, O Lord, gives me hope from day to day.

Doing Your holy will, O Lord, gives me mental powers.

Doing Your holy will, O Lord, makes me happy.

Doing Your holy will, O Lord, help me to love everybody.

Doing Your holy will, O Lord, encourages me to love you more and more.

Doing Your holy will, O Lord, is 24 hours, around the clock.

Doing Your holy will, O Lord, is stronger than any man in this world.

Doing Your holy will, O Lord, is higher than the highest mountain.

Doing Your holy will, O Lord, is more beautiful than the lily in the valley.

Doing Your holy will, O Lord, shines brighter than the sun.

Doing Your holy will, O Lord, is from everlasting to everlasting.

Doing Your holy will, O Lord, is everything that I need.

Doing Your holy will, O Lord, is better than anything in this world.

Doing Your holy will, O Lord, protects me from doing my will.

Doing Your holy will, O Lord, gives me the strength to get through the day.

Doing Your holy will, O Lord, is the best thing that can happen in my life.

Doing Your holy will, O Lord, causes death to move farther away from me.

Doing Your holy will, O Lord, is never a lost cause to me or anyone else.

Doing Your holy will, O Lord, is not only for me to do on earth but also for me to do in heaven too.

Doing Your holy will, O Lord, lets my enemies see that You, O Lord, are for me and not against me.

Doing Your holy will, O Lord, helps me to make this world a better place to live in.

Living an Honest Life

Don't disrespect people. You don't want anyone to disrespect you.

Don't cheat people. You don't want anyone to cheat you.

Don't lie to people. You don't want anyone to tell you a lie.

Live an honest life, as if it was your last day to live.

Don't be rude to people. You don't want anyone to be rude to you.

Don't talk bad to people. You don't want anyone to talk bad to you.

Don't steal from people. You don't want anyone to steal from you.

Live an honest life, as if it was your last day to live.

Don't kill people. You don't want anyone to kill you.

Don't deceive people. You don't want anyone to deceive you.

Don't hurt people. You don't want anyone to hurt you.

Live an honest life, as if it was your last day to live.

Don't be unfair to people. You don't want anyone to be unfair to you.

Don't use people. You don't want anyone to use you.

Don't upset people. You don't want anyone to upset you.

Live an honest life, as if it was your last day to live.

Don't treat people bad. You don't want anyone to treat you bad.

Don't give people an evil eye look. You don't want anyone to give you an evil eye look.

Don't assume things about people. You don't want anyone to assume anything about you.

Don't manipulate people. You don't want anyone to manipulate you.

Live an honest life, as if it was your last day to live.

Don't tease people. You don't want people to tease you.

Don't mock people. You don't want anyone to mock you.

Don't curse at people. You don't want anyone to curse at you.

Don't hate people. You don't want anyone to hate you.

Treat people the way that you want to be treated.

Live your life as if it was your last day to live.

When Jesus lived here on Earth, He always lived an honest life.

Jesus treated everybody right.

Jesus spoke the truth to everybody.

Jesus loved everybody.

Jesus set the right example for you and me to live an honest life.

The devil hates to be honest.

The devil is a thief, a murderer and a liar every day.

You and I can live an honest life through Jesus Christ, who never said a dishonest word and never did anything dishonest when He lived here on Earth.

It Didn't Happen Overnight

Making a lot of good choices in my life didn't happen overnight.

Eating a lot of the right foods didn't happen overnight.

Not smoking cigarettes didn't happen overnight.

Not drinking alcohol didn't happen overnight.

Not fornicating didn't happen overnight

Telling no more lies didn't happen overnight

Not being proud anymore didn't happen overnight.

Not doing foolish things didn't happen overnight.

Not talking foolishly didn't happen overnight.

Not making a lot of mistakes didn't happen overnight.

Wising up a lot didn't happen overnight.

Speaking a lot of good words didn't happen overnight

Doing a lot of good deeds didn't happen overnight.

Making more mature decisions didn't happen overnight.

Being more careful didn't happen overnight.

Being more tactful didn't happen overnight.

Being more loving didn't happen overnight.

Being more understanding didn't happen overnight.

Being smarter didn't happen overnight.

Believing in Jesus Christ didn't happen overnight.

Loving and obeying Jesus didn't happen overnight.

Making Jesus my choice didn't happen overnight.

Putting my trust in Jesus didn't happen overnight.

Being humble unto Jesus didn't happen overnight.

Denying myself and picking up my cross to follow Jesus didn't happen overnight.

Being stronger in the Lord Jesus Christ didn't happen overnight.

It didn't happen overnight that the Lord brought me this far for me to be saved in Him.

Oh Lord, You know

Oh Lord, You know what to allow me to go through to mold me and shape me into being faithful unto You.

Oh Lord, You know what to allow me to go through to help me to be obedient unto You.

Oh Lord, You know what to allow me to go through to help me to be humble unto You.

Oh Lord, You know what to allow me to go through to help me to hold onto You.

Oh Lord, you know what to allow me to go through to help me keep my eyes on You.

Oh Lord, you know me so much better than I will ever know myself.

Oh Lord, you know me so much better and anyone else will ever know me.

Oh Lord, you know where I have been and You know where I'm going.

Oh Lord, you know all of my thoughts.

Oh Lord, You know all of my mind.

Oh Lord, You know all of my words.

Oh Lord, You know all of my actions.

Oh Lord, you know all of my heart.

Oh Lord, I will never know myself like You know me.

Oh Lord, no one else will ever know me like You know me.

Oh Lord, You know all of my mistakes.

Oh Lord, You know all of my flaws.

Oh Lord, You know all of my failures.

Oh Lord, You know all of my rejections.

Oh Lord, You know all of my fears.

Oh Lord, You know all of my heartaches.

Oh Lord, You know all of my grief.

Old Lord, You know me all of my life-long days.

Oh Lord, You know all of the ups and downs in my life.

Oh Lord, You know all of my weaknesses.

Oh Lord, You know all my sins.

Oh Lord, You know all of my burdens.

Oh Lord, You know all of my works.

Oh Lord, You know all of my motives.

Oh Lord, You know all of my intentions.

Oh Lord, there is nothing that You don't know.

Oh Lord, You know what I will think before I think it.

Oh Lord, You know what I will say before I say it.

Oh Lord, You know what I will do before I do it.

Oh Lord, You know all of my pain.

Oh Lord, You know all of my joy.

Oh Lord, You know all of my victories.

Oh Lord, You know all of me, inside and out.

Oh Lord, You know all of my past.

Oh Lord, You know all of my present.

Oh Lord, You know all of my future.

Oh Lord, You know my destiny so much more than I will ever know and so much more than anyone else will ever know.

Eternal Life To Look Forward To

Just because we are Christians, it doesn't mean that we won't go through any hardships in life.

We Christians will go through some disappointments, but thanks to Jesus Christ we have eternal life to look forward to.

We Christians will go through some heartaches, but thanks to Jesus Christ we have eternal life to look forward to.

We Christians will go through some grieving, but we have eternal life to look forward to.

We Christians will get sick, but we have eternal life to look forward to.

We Christians will be hated, but we have eternal life to look forward to.

We Christians will be lied about, but we have eternal life and look forward to.

We Christians will be looked down upon, but we have eternal life to look forward to.

We Christians will be judged, but we have eternal life to look forward to.

We Christians will be treated badly, but we have eternal life to look forward to.

We Christians will be talked about in negative ways, but we have eternal life to look forward to.

We Christians will make some mistakes, but we have eternal life to look forward to.

We Christians will die, but we have eternal life to look forward to thanks to our Lord and Savior Jesus Christ.

We Christians have eternal life to look forward to for being saved in Jesus Christ.

We Christians will go through some hard times in our lives, but we can look forward to eternal life that the non-Christian people of the world can't look forward to.

We Christians will go through some injustice, but we have eternal life to look forward to.

We Christians will go through some rejections, but we have eternal life to look forward to.

We Christians will go through some biases, but we have eternal life to look forward to.

All the bad things that we Christians will go through for Jesus's name's sake will one day soon seal us to go to heaven with Jesus when He comes back again.

In the Name of Jesus

In the name of Jesus, Satan get thee behind me with your temptations of grudges.

In the name of Jesus, Satan get thee behind me with your temptations of lust.

In the name of Jesus, Satan get thee behind me with your temptations of jealousy.

In the name of Jesus, Satan get thee behind me with your temptations of discontentment.

In the name of Jesus, Satan get thee behind me with your temptations of gossip.

In the name of Jesus, Satan get thee behind me with your temptations of manipulation.

In the name of Jesus, Satan get thee behind me with your temptations of greed.

In the name of Jesus, Satan get thee behind me with your temptations of idols.

In the name of Jesus, Satan get thee behind me with your temptations of gluttony.

In the name of Jesus, Satan get thee behind me with your temptations of intemperance.

In the name of Jesus, Satan get thee behind me with your temptations of lying.

In the name of Jesus, Satan get thee behind me with your temptations of fear.

In the name of Jesus, Satan get thee behind me with your temptations of depression.

In the name of Jesus, Satan get thee behind me with your temptations of stress.

In the name of Jesus, Satan get thee behind me with your temptations of strife.

In the name of Jesus, Satan get thee behind me with your temptations of deception.

In the name of Jesus, Satan get thee behind me with your temptations of prejudice.

In the name of Jesus, Satan get thee behind me with your temptations of hatred.

In the name of Jesus, Satan get thee behind me with your temptations of anger.

In the name of Jesus, Satan get thee behind me with your temptations of violence.

In the name of Jesus, Satan get thee behind me with your temptations of disobedience.

In the name of Jesus, Satan get thee behind me with your temptations of vanity.

In the name of Jesus, Satan get thee behind me with your temptations of rebellion.

In the name of Jesus, Satan get thee behind me with your temptations of partiality.

In the name of Jesus, Satan get thee behind me with your temptations of unrighteousness.

In the name of Jesus, Satan get thee behind me with your temptations of self-righteousness.

In the name of Jesus, Satan get thee behind me with your temptations of selfishness.

Jesus is Like

Jesus is like a good pair of shoes that I can wear to walk through this hard-concrete world.

Jesus is like a coat that I can put on to keep my soul warm in this cold world.

Jesus is like an umbrella over me to keep my life dry in this sin-soaked world.

Jesus is like clothes on my body to keep me covered up in His righteousness in this naked, unrighteous world.

Jesus is like water that I can drink to keep me from getting spiritually dehydrated in this dry-well world.

Jesus is like good healthy food that I can eat to keep me spiritually healthy in this spiritually unhealthy world.

Jesus is like a beautiful pathway that I can use to walk safely through this spiritually dead-end world.

Jesus is like a beautiful, warm, sunny day for me to enjoy in this spiritually dark and cloudy world.

Jesus is like a big, tall tree that can give me plenty of shade in this spiritual heatwave world.

Jesus is like a quiet night where I can get a good night's sleep in this spiritually loud mob world.

Jesus is like the fresh air that I breathe in this spiritually polluted air world.

Jesus is like honey that tastes so sweet to me in this bitter and sour world.

Jesus is like good medicine I can take in this spiritually sick world.

Jesus is like a crystal-clear window glass for me to see through in this spiritually spotted-up world.

Jesus is like a ship sailing on a peaceful sea that I can use to reach the seashore in this shipwrecked world.

Jesus is like a gold mine where I can get spiritually rich in this spiritually poor world.

Jesus is like an aircraft pilot who can fly me to heaven one day over this world that will come to an end one day.

Jesus is like a surgeon who operates on my heart and removes my sins in this sinful world.

Jesus is like a perimeter set up to protect me with a crossfire of spiritual bullets in this spiritually combative world.

Jesus Can

Jesus can give you peace of mind when this world tries to take away your peace of mind.

Jesus can take away your stress when this world stresses you out.

Jesus can give you victory when this world tries to cause you to fail.

Jesus can give you unspeakable joy when this world tries to make you depressed.

Jesus can never fail you, but this world can fail you.

Jesus can give you everlasting love when this world stops loving you.

Jesus can give you everlasting life when this world tries to shorten your life.

Jesus can save you from your sins when this world tries to cause you to be lost in your sins.

Jesus can forgive you of your sins when this world tries to condemn you for your sins.

Jesus can help you to overcome your weaknesses when this world tries to cause you to get weaker and not overcome your weaknesses.

Jesus can give you abundance in life when this world tries to give you trouble in your life.

Jesus can give you contentment when this world tries to cause you to be greedy for worldly gain.

Jesus can give you everlasting truth when this world tries to give you so many lies.

Jesus can give you freedom when this world tries to keep you in bondage.

Jesus can give you justice when this world tries to give you injustice.

Jesus can give you a well mind when this world tries to give you an ill mind.

Jesus can give you a good life when this world tries to give you a horrible life.

Jesus can give you blessings when this world tries to give you curses.

Jesus can give you favor when this world tries to give you misfortune.

Jesus can give you a contrite heart when this world tries to harden your heart.

Jesus can renew your life when this world tries to cause you to live your life in sin.

Jesus can make your burdens as light as a feather when this world tries to make your burdens heavy.

Jesus can give you hope when this world tries to cause you to lose hope.

Jesus can answer your prayers when this world turns its back on you.

Jesus can be for you when this world is against you.

Jesus can let you live to reach old age when this world tries to take your life away from you every day.

What Have We Black People Done to You White People?

What have we black people done to you white people?

Many of us black people are peaceful people.

Many of us black people show some love to you white people.

Many of us black people try our best to get along with you white people.

Many of us black people do not judge you white people.

Many of us black people like you white people.

Many of us black people admire you white people.

Many of us black people will never harm you white people.

Many of us black people like our own black people.

You white people don't have to be afraid of every black man.

What have we black people done to you white people to make many of you judge us like many of you do?

What have we black people done to you white people to make many of you hate us like many of you do?

Many of us black people would like to have some good white friends.

Many of us black people don't hold any grudges against you white people, regardless of your many white ancestors who put our black ancestors into slavery.

Many of us black people like the way you white people carry yourselves.

Many of us black people like the way you white people look.

Many of us black people like the way other black people carry themselves.

Many of us black people like the way we black people look.

What have we black people done to you white people to make many of you so prejudiced against us as many of you are?

Many of us black people are good to you white people.

Many of us black people will not do evil things to you white people.

Us good black people don't feel good about bad black people who make all of us black people look bad.

Many of us black people don't have anything against you white people.

Many of us black people try our best to get along with you white people.

Many of us black people do not envy you white people.

Many of us black people don't think badly about you white people.

What have we black people done to you white people to make many of you look down on us like many of you do?

Many of us black people learn a lot of good things from you white people.

Many of us black people also learn a lot of good things from our own black people.

Many of us black people know that there are a lot of good white people.

Many of us black people appreciate good white people.

Many of us black people know that many white people are brilliant.

Many of us black people know that many of our black people are also brilliant.

Many of us black people do not hate white people.

Many of us black people are honest with white people.

What have we black people done to you white people to make many of you treat us so unfairly as many of you do?

Many of us black people will treat you white people fairly.

Many of us black people will treat you white people right.

Many of us black people will treat our own black people right.

Many of us black people will put up with you white people's bad ways.

Many of us black people will put up with our own black people's bad ways.

Many of us black people will not put you white people down.

Many of us black people will not put our own black people down.

What have we black people done to you white people to make many of you oppress us the way many of you do?

Many of us black people will not plot anything against you white people.

Many of us black people will not plot anything against our own black people.

Many of us black people will listen to good advice from you white people.

Many of us black people will listen to good advice from our own black people.

Many of us black people will not give white people a hard time.

Many of us black people will not give our own black people a hard time.

What have we black people done to you white people that makes you disrespect us like many of you do?

Many of us black people do not disrespect you white people.

Many of us black people do not disrespect our own black people.

Many of us black people do trust many of you white people.

Many of us black people do trust many of our own black people.

Many of us black people's hearts are touched by many of you white people.

Many of us black people's hearts are touched by many of our own black people.

Many of us black people do not break under the pressure of you white people.

Many of us black people do not break under the pressure of our own black people.

What have we black people done to you white people that makes many of you want to kill us like many of you do?

Many of us black people will not joke about you white people.

Many of us black people do not joke about our own black people.

Many of us black people believe in Jesus Christ, just like many of you white people do.

Many of us black people are saved in Jesus Christ, just like many of you white people are.

Many of us black people will go to heaven, just like many of you white people who will go to heaven.

What have we black people done to you white people that makes many of you want to talk bad about us and go out of your way to not get to know us?

Many of us black people want to get to know you white people, especially you good white people.

Many of us black people admire the talents and skills that you white people have.

Many of us black people admire the talents and skills our own black people have.

Many of us black people love everybody, regardless of their race, creed or culture.

Many of us black people are peaceful and humble people.

Many of us black people are respectful people.

Many of us black people are strong and joyful people.

Many of us black people will accept you white people for who you are.

Many of us black people know that many of your own white people don't treat you right all of the time.

Many of us black people will stand up for what is right with you white people.

Many of us black people will stand up for what is right with own black people.

What have we black people done to you white people that makes many of you want to segregate yourselves away from us black people?

Many of us black people will look up to many of you white people.

Many of us black people will look up to many of our own black people.

Many of us black people will risk our lives to save you white people.

Many of us black people will risk our lives to save our own black people.

Many of us black people appreciate every race, creed and culture of people.

Many of us black people see beauty in every race, creed and culture of people.

Many of us black people know that God is in every race, creed and culture of people.

What have we black people done to you white people that makes many of you do not want to respect us black people?

The Black Will

The black will penetrated through the iron wall of 400 years of slavery.

The black will is strong, like hurricane winds.

The black will has blown down many years of segregation.

The black will is like a high mountain cliff where people stand on the edge and do not fall off into hopelessness.

The black will is like a light at the end of the dark tunnel of inequality.

The black will is like the deep oceans.

The black will is deep in perseverance.

The black will is like a peaceful river that flows.

The black church has flowed peacefully in this troubled nation.

The black will is like a sunny, warm day.

The black will shines its warmth through the police violence and brutality on black people.

The black will is like the full, white moon shining so mysterious all night long.

The black will shines so mysterious with endurance so other races of people can see that we black people are survivors in this world.

The black will is like all the stars sparkling in the night.

Our black ancestors birthed our black people to be here today so we can sparkle in the night of injustice.

The black will is like a fruit tree planted near the water.

Through the many years in this nation, we black people have grown many fruits of talents, skills, wisdom and knowledge to help make this nation great today.

The black will is like the deep valleys that run between the hills and mountains.

We black people are down in the deep valleys of not getting all the privileges that this nation only gives to those who are favored to be privileged.

The black will is like a cruise ship on the ocean waters.

Our black ancestors cruised through the rugged waves of 400 years of slavery so us black people could enjoy our freedom today.

Things in our world are not like it was back in their day, regardless of the prejudice that is going on.

The black will is like the rooster that crowed at Peter for denying Jesus Christ three times.

The black will crows at prejudiced people who deny Jesus and hate people, no matter what their skin color is.

God's will gave birth to the black will and let it grow up strong over 400 years of slavery.

The black will found favor with God for us black people to not ever be extinct in this world.

The black will is like the Grand Canyon that is very massive.

We black people are very massive in numbers all around the world.
The black will is like a published book.

Our black lives are like a book for all the world to read and see that our black lives are a best-seller.

The black will has been through rugged terrain and disappointment.

The black will has been through the wilderness of heartaches.
The black will has been through the title waves of being misunderstood.

The black will has been through the earthquakes of hardships.

The black will today is going through the heatwaves of being treated unfairly.

The black will today is going through the snow blizzards of being disrespected.

The black will today is going through the polluted waters of violence.

The black will today is breathing in and out the polluted air of people who are not concerned about what's going on with us black people.

The black will is a great thing for all of us black people to always hold onto because the black will is the choices that every black man, woman, boy and girl can make for being mature in one's right mind.

Our black ancestors made their choices in their black will that God gave to them.

They chose to keep on living the best way that they could through years of slavery.

The black will has also affected many prejudiced people and made them feel guilty about treating black people badly.

The black will is very popular with the angels in heaven, but the black will is not popular with prejudiced people.

The Black Dream

The black dream is for oppression to end upon black people.

The black dream is for equal opportunity to come alive for all black people.

The black dream is for justice for all black people.

The black dream is for no economic slavery upon black people.

The black dream is for all black people to have the privilege to buy a house.

The black dream is for black people to be treated right by all people of another race.

The black dream is for all black people to prosper.

The black dream is for all black people to not be looked down upon.

The black dream is for all black people to forgive white people.

The black dream is for all black people to love ourselves, regardless of what prejudiced people say or do.

The black dream is for all black people to love being black.

The black dream is for all black people to treat everybody right.

The black dream is for all black people to come out of the wilderness of inequality.

The black dream is for all black people to come out of their dark cave of silence and not let violence and brutality upon black people keep going on.

The black dream is for all black people to turn back to God.

The black dream is for all black people to know that they are somebody who can choose to do good things in this world.

The black dream is for all black people to move on beyond prejudiced people.

The black dream is for all black people to know the past dark days of 400 years of slavery are over and use that knowledge to work for justice and liberty today.

The black dream is for all black people to show prejudiced people that we are not like them who love to hate black people and brown people.

The black dream is a very powerful dream that will greatly disturb prejudiced people who can't kill the black dream.

The black dream is very real in many black people who will protect it to get justice.

The black dream is very real in many black people who are bold and stand up for change.

The black dream is very real in many black people who live their lives for civil rights.

The black dream is very real in many black people who won't let black history die and be forgotten like there was no 400 years of black slavery in this nation.

The black dream is very real in many black Christians who love and forgive their prejudiced enemies.

The black dream is like the full, white moonlight shining all night long.

The black dream is like a beautiful rainbow arching across the sky after the rain.

The black dream is like the sunlight melting the snow after a snow blizzard is over.

The black dream is like the beautiful flowers that bloom in the springtime.

The black dream is like clean water running from the spring.

The black dream is for all black people to be healed from prejudice.

The black dream is for all black people to come together to make this world a better place to live in.

The black dream is for all black people to dream with our eyes open wide and see that we are making a difference in educating this nation so others are not ignorant about who we are.

The black dream is for all black people to dream big so that we can be understood by other races of people so they won't judge us all to be criminals.

The black dream is for all black people to dream with their eyes opened wide to see that true freedom is loving God and keeping His Commandments.

The black dream is for all great and small black people to look deep within themselves and let Jesus Christ in to help them to not be prejudiced against another race of people or our own black people.

Many of our own black people are prejudiced against one another.

Some dark-skinned black people don't like light-skinned black people.

Some light-skinned black people don't like dark-skinned black people.

Many of the brown-skinned black people are caught in the middle.

The black dream is a great dream that all black people can hold onto for as long as we live.

Prejudiced people can't take away our black dream.

Our black dream is very real to us every day.

Our black dream is a dream that God gave to all of us black people.

The black dream is for all of us black people to dream with our eyes opened wide so we can see that God didn't bring us this far to let us down and allow the past to repeat itself.

God gave us a great dream that prejudiced people don't respect and will mock.

God has shined His sunlight on our black dream and our black existence all around the world.

Our black dream is a dream that we black people can see with our eyes open wide so our black dream can be real and active in our black lives.

When we lay down to sleep, we will have some dreams until we wake up and those dreams fade away, but our black dream will never fade away because it is very real in our daily living.

Our black dream began with our black ancestors, who never gave up their black dream and passed it down to us black people today.

Our black ancestors had a dream of a better day for you and me, and we need to make sure that dream was not in vain.

The black dream is the vision of the past, present and future for all of us black people who put God first in our lives and give Him the glory and praise for our black dream.

There Is Nothing Good About The Devil

There is nothing good about stealing.

There is nothing good about killing.

There is nothing good about lying.

There is nothing good about the devil, who lives to steal.

There is nothing good about the devil, who loves to kill.

There is nothing good about the devil, who loves to lie.

There's nothing good about ruining people's good names.

There is nothing good about manipulating people.

There is nothing good about treating people badly.

There is nothing good about the devil, who loves to ruin people's good names.

There is nothing good about the devil, who loves to manipulate people.

There is nothing good about the devil, who loves to treat people badly.

There is nothing good about showing favoritism.

There is nothing good about being proud.

There is nothing good about disrespecting people.

There's nothing good about the devil, who loves to show favoritism.

There is nothing good about the devil, who is proud.

There's nothing good about the devil, who loves to disrespect people.

There is nothing good about shooting people down with words.

There is nothing good about throwing indirect words at people.

There's nothing good about using people.

There is nothing good about the devil, who loves to shoot people down with words.

There is nothing good about the devil, who loves to throw indirect words at people.

There is nothing good about the devil, who loves to use people.

There is nothing good about abusing people.

There is nothing good about saying one thing and doing another thing.

There is nothing good about telling lies about people.

There's nothing good about the devil, who loves to abuse people.

There is nothing good about the devil, who will say one thing and do another thing.

There is nothing good about the devil, who loves to tell lies about people.

There is nothing good about pretending.

There is nothing good about cheating.

There's nothing good about being selfish.

There's nothing good about the devil, who loves to pretend.

There is nothing good about the devil, who loves to cheat.

There is nothing good about the devil, who is selfish.

There is nothing good about causing people to sin against the Lord.

There is nothing good about laughing at people's sins.

There is nothing good about making wrong things look like they're right things to say and do.

There is nothing good about putting anything above the Lord.

There is nothing good about the devil, who loves to cause people to sin against the Lord.

There is nothing good about the devil, who loves to laugh at people's sins.

There is nothing good about the devil, who loves to make wrong things look like right things to say and do.

There is nothing good about the devil, who loves to put himself above the Lord.

There is nothing good about wanting what belongs to other people.

There is nothing good about deceiving people.

There is nothing good about flattering people.

There is nothing good about the devil, who wants what belongs to others.

There is nothing good about the devil, who loves to deceive people.

There is nothing good about the devil, who loves to flatter people.

There is nothing good about hating people.

There's nothing good about the devil, who hates people.

There is nothing good about the devil, who hates God.

Make Something Good Out of Something Bad

The devil loves to make things bad for us, but the Lord can make something good out of something bad.

You and I can't make something good out of something bad, because the bad will usually get the best of us.

When we see the bad, we don't see what good can come from it.

The Lord always sees what good can come from the bad, because the Lord knows how to make something good out of something bad.

We can see the bad things that many people do.

We can hear about the bad things that many people do.

Only the Lord can always use something bad to help us wise up, which is surely something good.

Only the Lord can always use something bad to help us see that we need to change our ways, and that is something good.

There is nothing good about doing something bad and no one can make excuses for this before the Lord, who can make something good out of something bad.

You and I will take the bad for what it is and not think twice about what good things can come out of the bad.

Most of the time, nothing good will come out of something bad.

The few times that something good comes out of something bad, it is the good that the Lord makes out of something bad.

Only the Lord can always see to bring something good out of something bad.

There is nothing that the Lord can't do.

The Lord can do all good things.

All good things come from the Lord.

The good that is in you and me is from the Lord.

No bad thing can stop the Lord from making something good out of something bad.

When something bad happens to you and me, we don't see anything good in it.

Only the Lord can always use bad things to help you and me to keep our faith in Him, which is a good thing.

We Christians Can't Sit Back

We Christians can't sit back and turn a blind eye toward injustice.

We Christians can't sit back and keep silent towards racism.

We Christians can't sit back and not go out and vote.

We Christians can't sit back and live our lives like nothing can affect us.

We Christians are supposed to stand up for justice.

We Christians are supposed to speak out against racism.

We Christians are supposed to go out to vote.

We Christians are supposed to be affected by the things going on in this world.

We Christians must stay in prayer and live right before the people of the world.

We Christians are supposed to set a good example and treat everybody right.

We Christians can't sit back and not use our spiritual gifts that Jesus Christ has given to us.

We Christians can't sit back and not be a witness of Jesus Christ.

We Christians must talk about Jesus Christ.

If the Lord has given you a gift to preach, you can't sit back and not preach about Jesus.

If the Lord has given you a gift to teach, you can't sit back and not teach about Jesus Christ.

If the Lord has given you a gift to write, you can't sit back and not write about Jesus Christ.

If the Lord has given you a gift to sing, you can't sit back and not sing songs about Jesus Christ.

If the Lord has given you a gift to make a lot of money, you can't sit back and not use your money to build up the Kingdom of Jesus Christ.

We Christians can't sit back and not speak the truth of God's holy word.

We Christians can't sit back and not watch what is going on in this world.

We Christian can't sit back and let time pass us by as if we have all the time in the world to be ready to go to heaven with Jesus Christ when He comes back again.

www.ingramcontent.com/pod-product-compliance
Lightning Source LLC
Chambersburg PA
CBHW071456070526
44578CB00001B/363